T0367195

THE PUTIN SYSTEM

THE PUTIN SYSTEM

AN OPPOSING VIEW

GRIGORY YAVLINSKY

Columbia University Press *New York*

Columbia University Press
Publishers Since 1893
New York Chichester, West Sussex
cup.columbia.edu

First published in the Russian as *Periferijnyj avtoritarizm: Kak i kuda prishla Rossija* (Moscow: Medium Publishers, 2015).

Library of Congress Cataloging-in-Publication Data
Names: I͡Avlinskiĭ, G. (Grigoriĭ), author.
Title: The Putin system : an opposing view / Grigory Yavlinsky.
Other titles: Periferiĭnyĭ avtoritarizm. English
Description: New York : Columbia University Press, [2018] |
Includes bibliographical references and index.
Identifiers: LCCN 2018028372 | ISBN 9780231190305 (cloth : acid-free paper) |
ISBN 9780231548823 (e-book)
Subjects: LCSH: Russia (Federation)—Politics and government—1991– |
Political culture—Russia (Federation) | Public administration—
Russia (Federation) | Authoritarianism—Russia (Federation)
Classification: LCC JN6695 .I36813 2018 | DDC 320.947—dc23
LC record available at https://lccn.loc.gov/2018028372

Columbia University Press books are printed on permanent
and durable acid-free paper.
Printed in the United States of America

Cover design: Noah Arlow

To my brave and faithful comrades-in-arms
in Russian politics

CONTENTS

PREFACE TO THE ENGLISH TRANSLATION

In this book, which builds upon more than a quarter century of my work as both a practicing politician and a scholarly analyst of Russia's development, I trace the resurgence and consolidation of authoritarian rule in post-Soviet Russia, first under Boris Yeltsin and then under his appointed successor, Vladimir Putin. I make the case for characterizing this regime as a peripheral one, and I do so for two major reasons. First, Russia continues to demonstrate economic and psychological dependence upon leading industrial powers, primarily the United States and Germany, which form the developed core of the world economic system. Second, many of Russia's policies stem from its leadership's resentment over being treated as a peripheral player, progressively marginalized within most international institutions and their decision-making on major global and regional issues.

I am fully aware that this argument appears to defy some of the basic elements of the narrative, put forth by mainstream Western media and by policy makers, about Russia as a powerful key player, not just in the world but also in American domestic affairs. In fact, I concur with the view that the Russian government's involvement in the affairs of the Western world in recent years may have had an impact on these societies that has been far from peripheral, even if it is impossible to quantify with precision. There is mounting evidence of the Kremlin's interference in the electoral process in the United States and Western Europe and in the inner workings of their democratic institutions, and that the Kremlin did so in support of radical right-wing forces and those seeking to undermine modern societies' foundational values of socioeconomic progress, social and racial justice, and opportunities for all. Whatever role the Russian government and its proxies played in the victory of Donald Trump in the US presidential elections in 2016—even though, in my analysis, any involvement was secondary to other, internal factors—the very fact of such interference was indeed central to US domestic political developments and foreign policy and hence to the evolution of the core of the world politico-economic system.

And yet, while the impact of Moscow's actions has definitely put Russia on the front pages of Western newspapers and in prime-time news, where it is likely to remain for the foreseeable future, it does not change the peripheral characteristics and position of Putin's Russia with regard to the developed industrial powers and the system of world governance that these sustain. In this regard, Russia is broadly comparable to North Korea: while Pyongyang's existential nuclear threat to the United States and its allies in the region, and potentially to the rest of the world, is central to the present-day international agenda, this in no way qualifies North Korea to be a part of the political core of the world system.

Granted, unlike North Korea, Russia is a veto-holding member of the UN Security Council and wields some influence in parts of the globe on the basis of its military power, and even more so for historical reasons. But, other than that, it is no longer a member of any club of developed industrial powers. And with a 2016 gross domestic product, according to its own official statistics, of less than $1.3 trillion—about 11 percent of the economy of mainland China and smaller than the gross domestic product of Italy or Brazil—Russia constitutes merely 1.8 percent of the world economy.

While Russia's economically peripheral position and its authoritarianism are historically interrelated, these are two distinct phenomena. They have different implications for the international system and call for different responses from the outside world. This authoritarianism, what I call "peripheral authoritarianism," is an issue on its own, but one that takes on a unique quality in light of Russia's economically peripheral status. At present, the combination of these two trends has resulted in antagonistic relations with key Western powers, perhaps the worst in Russia's modern history, but it doesn't have to continue in this fashion. Russia may be peripheral or semiperipheral in the world's economy, but it does not have to be ruled by an inward-looking, xenophobic government whose crony capitalists park their wealth overseas, in the banks and real estate of the developed core countries, while their government hypocritically demonizes and denounces Western ways of life from Russian television screens.

The positive aspects of international relations in the period of détente, during perestroika, and during the first post-Soviet years remind us that Russia is by no means inherently anti-Western and that a different type of relations is a realistic possibility. It is essential for American readers to keep this in mind and to not accept uncritically the media's stereotypes of the Russian people as falling in line with authoritarian Russian propaganda. This stereotyping ultimately harms, first and foremost, those who are working toward better Russian–American relations and toward a Russia that, politically, would be an integral part of Europe.

It is equally important to realize that a Western response to the Kremlin's actions that heavily relies on sanctions and other hard-line solutions intended to defang Russia's authoritarian regime by driving it even further into the global economic periphery is ineffective at best. The latest *World Wealth Report* shows that, from 2015 to 2016, the number of millionaires in Russia and their total wealth grew by 20 percent—faster than the total for the world—and the growth continued in 2017, though at a lower rate.[1] And such a hard-line approach is highly likely to backfire, by strengthening the regime and hardening nationalistic support for its foreign ventures.

The paradox at play is that while Russia's peripheral economic position vis-à-vis the developed world is unexceptional and is a matter of concern to Russia only, its political system of peripheral authoritarianism, which is built upon this economic base, has proven to be a significant, if not the driving force behind Russia's major conflicts and crises in various parts of the world. Some of these situations have an overtly military component (as in Ukraine and Syria), while others, such as those caused by the explosive rise of the radical right in American and European politics, are of a different nature. But all of them are deeply affecting the political systems of the developed "core"—not only tangentially, through the flow of refugees and increased military engagements, but now also directly, by contributing to political upheavals in the United States and Western Europe.

Thus, the apparent attempts by the Putin government or its proxies to intervene in the electoral politics of the developed core of the world system—through hacking computer systems of Western political institutions, leaking their internal information to cause damage to specific candidates (first and foremost to Hillary Clinton) and providing various forms of support for the radical or even not-so-radical right—represents a rather brazen effort to take revenge for the peripheral position and status that Putin's Russia holds within the political system of global governance. This is the purpose of the Kremlin's "active measures" to discredit basic European values and to strengthen isolationist and destructive forces in Western societies.

Whether this attempted revenge will be successful—that is, whether it will lead to a long-term core-periphery realignment favorable to Putin's Russia—is primarily an issue of internal vulnerabilities of the core, of the US and Western European democracies, which are exposed through the weakening of their democratic institutions and value systems. This weakening has been a matter of concern for quite a while, as it increasingly fuels global uncertainty and chaos, a crisis of confidence in the future of our world, and even apocalyptic expectations in place of a compelling vision of sustainable development.

There is plenty of evidence that this weakening is rooted primarily in the decay of civil society institutions, as seen in the declining influence and shrinking material resources of labor unions, nonprofits, local self-government, political parties, and so on. In recent decades, this retrenchment of civil society has been described and analyzed from different perspectives by leading political thinkers, starting with Harvard University's Robert Putnam, in his now classic work *Bowling Alone*.[2] There are many reasons to agree with those who see the retrenchment as caused by dramatically rising economic inequality and the decline of the middle class, unleashed by the neoliberal economic agenda that spread like fire from the United Kingdom and the United States to what was then still the Soviet bloc and that has dominated since then. This, in turn, resulted from the triumph of the ideology of self-regulating markets and the allegedly spontaneous social order generated by them, which is devoid of any value judgment about their social impact.

To summarize, the weakening of Western democratic institutions is a long-term trend that emerged well before Moscow's interference in Western countries' internal politics. Actually, the weakening made the interference possible, even though, in a vicious circle of sorts, Moscow's interference may have exacerbated the damage to democratic institutions and values.

Thus, without a major awakening of Western societies and their power holders, the impact of such interference may go far deeper than we can imagine today. Not only do Western countries need to be cognizant of the dangers posed by even the possibility of a peripheral authoritarian regime interfering with their electoral processes, but also, no less importantly, they must be aware of their own internal vulnerabilities vis-à-vis the resurgence of authoritarian tribalism fueled by glaring economic inequality. In this case, the corrosion of the institutions of national and global governance can become potentially irreversible, undermining our ability to generate rational solutions to life-and-death issues of the day, from military defense to the planetary threat of human-generated climate change. Meanwhile, the disintegration of the US-led unipolar world order and the failure of multipolarity increase the likelihood of a major war with catastrophic consequences for our civilization.

I am deeply convinced that the single most powerful weapon of Western self-defense against this scenario is the resilience of the West's democratic institutions and their ability to prevail over their own internal threats of authoritarian degeneration. One of the remaining key differences between the core and the periphery, in this instance, is that the core has internal resources for such a transformation and revival, while any similar developments in a peripheral or semiperipheral country like Russia depend upon the impulses from the core. Today, therefore, the possibility of a less authoritarian, less xenophobic, and overall less dangerous Russia primarily hinges upon the resurgence of democratic political and civic institutions in the West and their ability to resist and to prevail in the ongoing struggle against their own domestic authoritarianism, neo-Nazism, racism, and other forms of bigotry and hate, and to subsequently transform the international agenda.

While democrats and progressives in Western societies are fighting this out, I urge them to not underestimate the additional strength that they will gain through substantive and meaningful relationships with their counterparts in countries such as Russia. Even though, with regard to their ability to change government policies, civil societies and antiauthoritarian forces in these countries are many times weaker than those in the West, they are by no means insignificant in terms of being able to generate or speed up their own societies' supportive responses to new signals coming from the core of the world system. Furthermore, some of these antiauthoritarian forces in peripheral and semiperipheral countries have developed unique practices of survival and nonviolent resistance. These practices may very well be both transferable and beneficial to American society, in response to the increasing attempts to transfer some of the features of Russia's peripheral authoritarianism to America's political landscape.

Russia's United Democratic Party Yabloko, which my colleagues and I founded in the fall of 1993, has been dedicated to serving as an antiauthoritarian force in Russian society. In fact, it is Russia's oldest currently functioning political entity to trace its origin and inspiration to the most recent round of Russia's attempts to rebuild itself and its civilizational identity as part and parcel of the European community of democratic nations. Thus, we envision Yabloko as poised to be a carrier and transmitter of active institutional memory about the achievements of the late

1980s and the early 1990s to the present and the next generation of politicians. The end of the Cold War created opportunities for improvement not only in Russia's domestic affairs but also in Russian–American relations—what was known back then, in American political parlance, as the "peace dividend." We strive to advocate for such opportunities to be resurrected, once Putin's rule ends, and to accomplish what must be done for both countries to take better advantage of these opportunities for mutual benefit.

Yabloko has continuously campaigned against the Kremlin's military interference in Ukraine and in Syria. We believe that, in both cases, the Kremlin has taken the wrong side of history and has been wasting Russia's precious human and financial resources. Likewise, we are firmly opposed to the Russian authorities' attempts to interfere with the domestic politics of the United States and Western European countries, whether through cyber warfare or by corrupting government officials and entire political parties, just as we objected to the instances of foreign interference in Russia's domestic politics, including in the 1996 presidential elections, on the side of Boris Yeltsin and his neoliberal market reformers—interference that partly paved the way for Putin's rise to power.

Yabloko's stand on Russian–Ukrainian relations is that Russian authorities must acknowledge that their annexation of Crimea violated international law. This is the key step toward any subsequent international negotiations that would ensure Ukraine's territorial integrity while safeguarding the interests of the population of Crimea in accordance with international law. Moscow also must stop supplying arms and equipment to secessionists in Eastern Ukraine and reach an agreement on the deployment of UN peacekeepers in the region.

We also urge the end of Russia's participation in Syria's civil war. Russian involvement has caused the loss of tens of thousands, if not hundreds of thousands, of peaceful Syrian lives, has fueled terrorism in the region, and has turned into a geopolitical trap for Russia itself. As part of our nationwide campaign to bring Russian servicemen home from the war zones, we held street actions in forty-seven cities and in thirty-eight out of Russia's ninety regions. More than one hundred thousand Russians have signed our petition to bring Russian troops back from Syria, and polls show that, during the five months of our campaign, the share of those polled who are opposed to Russia's participation in this war has grown from 34 percent to 49 percent—and we know that many more do not disclose their views to pollsters out of fear. Meanwhile, Yabloko's representatives in regional legislative bodies have introduced a federal bill that would limit presidential war powers and have been urging these regional parliaments to use their right of federal legislative initiative to move this bill forward.

On March 18, 2018, presidential elections were held in Russia. With Vladimir Putin and his inner circle in nearly total control of the entirety of the country's government apparatus—the infamous "power vertical"—and of every significant financial resource that could be used for political purposes, the outcome seemed to be predetermined. Yet it was not automatic, given that, even under these circumstances, open support for democratic opposition, not only in its traditional centers such as Moscow and Saint Petersburg but also in such places as Pskov and Sakhalin, was quite considerable. The extent of this support and the potential for its further rapid growth have been revealed by the results of the elections to local councils, held on September 10, 2017. In Moscow local councils, we were proud to see that Yabloko has become the second-largest political force after Putin's United Russia, increasing its representation more than tenfold by gaining 176 seats, or nearly 12 percent of the total number. And, symbolically, we won all the seats in the district in which Vladimir Putin is registered to vote.

The goal of the authorities during the 2018 election was to secure for Putin the kind of landslide after which any democratic opposition can be totally obliterated and ignored, so that his successor can be picked and groomed without any undesirable influences from outside of the Kremlin. This required an array of means that, to the best of our knowledge, ranged from trivial fraud in places like Moscow to injecting fake candidacies of pop stars and other patently unqualified contenders, which made Putin look like the bedrock of sanity by comparison.

As Yabloko's candidate in the 2018 presidential election, my primary goal for our democratic alternative in these elections was to wage the kind of substantive domestic as well as international campaign that could, in spite of the Kremlin's control over Russia's mass media, generate some constraints upon the possibility of a further transformation of Russia's authoritarian regime in a decidedly totalitarian and militaristic direction over the next six years of Putin's fourth presidential term. To achieve this, Yabloko openly spoke about this threat, openly campaigned for the end of Russia's military interference and "hybrid warfare" in Ukraine and Syria, and openly denounced the Kremlin's intrusion in the political processes in Western countries on the side of antidemocratic forces that are sowing division, violence, and hate.

To ensure the success of this strategy, which extends far beyond the election, it is essential for the Western public and its political class to pay attention to liberals in Russia and their struggle. Indeed, listening and engaging in a continuous dialogue is arguably the most effective, and perhaps even the only realistic way to support them, given the draconian legal restrictions on all other forms of foreign political involvement in Russia. Such a dialogue is presently impeded not only by the rising economic and political barriers on both sides but also by the drastic de-intellectualization of politics in both Russia and Western countries and the ensuing disintegration of the universal language of mutual understanding across cultures and political systems. Part and parcel of this decay is the decreasing amount of high-quality translations into English of conceptual political writings in the languages of non-English-speaking countries, such as Russia.

If we want the antiauthoritarian forces in Russia and in the West to strengthen each other and to amplify each other's voices in our native languages, we must break through these barriers by encouraging more translations of original political works that effectively convey our respective messages to each other while preserving the authenticity and the context of the original. My main aim in bringing the present translation of this book to an English-speaking audience is to contribute to such a cross-cultural dialogue.

ACKNOWLEDGMENTS

I am grateful to my colleagues, all brilliant and honest intellectuals, for the constant discussions in which this book was born: Vitaly Shvydko, Andrei Kosmynin, Victor Kogan-Yasny, and Eugenia Dillendorf.

My special appreciation to Antonina and Jean-Claude Bouis, without whom this volume would not exist.

Dmitri Glinski's wonderful translation evinces a deep understanding of the book's substance, and I am extremely grateful to him for that. I thank Igor Yakovlev, who helped me in the organization of the book's translation.

I also thank the anonymous reviewers who recommended this book for publication for the credit of trust they expressed in me. My words of thanks go to the Columbia University Press team for their attentive and professional handling of the manuscript.

In conclusion, I would like to thank my beloved family for their unselfish love and support. They have made contributions to the book in a variety of ways.

THE PUTIN SYSTEM

1

THE POLITICAL SYSTEM OF PUTIN'S RUSSIA AND ITS SIGNIFICANCE FOR WORLD AFFAIRS

At the turn of the millennium, in the wake of a rapid and, in many ways, catastrophic collapse of the Soviet political and economic system, a peculiar social and economic formation became reality in the "new" Russia. What I am talking about are not any particular events or even trends that have been present in Russian political and economic life over the past two decades but rather the overall framework of entrenched economic and social relationships that now exist there. Having emerged gradually over this period of time, this problematic framework is now entrenched and normalized in Russia. This framework is what the Marxist tradition used to call the "social order"—a set of substantive relationships that shape the texture of social life for the long term, regardless of what people themselves say or think about these relationships.

In examining the problematic aspects of the post-Soviet Russian social order, my primary focus (perhaps because of my mind-set and range of interests) was on the economic aspects of the system, which I believe are a major cause of Russia's current ills. To the extent possible, and based on my experience, I sought to grasp and to outline, in more or less scholarly terms, the property ownership and management relationships in post-Soviet

Russia. For all the high drama of Russia's political conflicts of the early 1990s, I believed, and continue to believe, that, in the end, this political turmoil was subordinate to those rather deep but not always evident economic developments that shaped the peculiar type of Russia's "new" capitalism. This capitalism emerged not so much as a result of, but rather against the wishes and calculations of nearly all the individuals and interest groups involved in its formation—forces that were frequently opposed to each other by their objective interests as well as by subjective aspirations.

But what exactly is the peculiar new capitalism in Russia? Let me outline briefly what I considered to be the main features of the Russian version of the post-Soviet economic system. I will then compare it to the current situation, and thus we shall see whether its principal elements are still relevant today.

The so-called reforms instituted after the fall of the Soviet Union were in fact not reforms at all but rather the Russian government's passive muddling along with the flow of uncontrolled developments. As a result of this, by the end of the 1990s we in Russia found ourselves hostage to an odd, eclectic system of economic relations. This system combined, in a bizarre fashion, elements of disparate phenomena, such as underdeveloped classic capitalism; institutions of modern postindustrial financial capitalism that were thoughtlessly added to the mix; relics of the Soviet-type administrative command economy and of the shadow economy embedded in it; semifeudal relationships rooted in Russia's pre-Soviet history; and, finally, trivial economic crime, such as bribes and fraud, as part of everyday business life.

Back then, no one was disputing this analysis in earnest. The debate was merely about the degrees to which all these disparate elements were present and about the immediate prospects for the system's further evolution. At the time, the so-called liberal reformers were, on the whole, optimistic and confident that this eclectic assemblage of different kinds of economic activities was merely a reflection of the economy's transitional character in the 1990s and that the spontaneous course of events was bringing Russia's economy closer to the mainstream of Western capitalism. For me, to the contrary, there was nothing in the state of Russia's economy at the time that would spontaneously propel it, as if on autopilot, toward a mature competitive capitalist economy.

I also noted that these disparate types of relationships in Russia's economy were not separated from each other by clear-cut boundaries. In other words, its economy was not neatly divided into segments dominated by specific types of organization, such as traditional, modern, postsocialist, and shadow economies. Instead, these ways of economic life were closely intertwined with each other, with the same economic sectors, the same companies, and even the same individuals pulled into these different economic orbits at the same time. As a result, each economic actor had to deal with a mixture of disparate norms, consisting of legal requirements, informal understandings, administrative dictates, violent crime (including violence that originated with government agencies), and a vast field of uncertainty, dominated by individual luck. In some of my writings, I characterized this state of affairs as an "economy of might and of happenstance."[1] In this kind of an economy, actors have to rely upon rules of the game that emerge outside of anyone's control, are rather volatile, and may change substantially, even within a single investment cycle, under the influence of changes in power relationships and of merely accidental factors.

Yet another thing that I considered to be very important was the assessment of the deeper roots of the Russian authorities' failure to get its economic house in order. Although it was true that Moscow ministerial cabinets in the 1990s made specific mistakes in their economic policies and failed to combat economic crime to the extent that was necessary, these were not the root causes of the failures of "transition." Rather, the primary cause was the poor understanding of the overall character of the social formation that emerged in the place of the Soviet economic system.

At the time of Russia's transition, I widely used the term "peripheral capitalism" to describe the country's economic system. I believe this reflects not only Russia's position in the global economy, of which the Russian economy became an inseparable part after the collapse of the Soviet-era "developed socialism," but also the characteristics of the new social system that emerged from its ruins. My point was that many aspects of these types of economic relationships, however regrettable, were a norm not just for Russia but also for the peripheral parts of world capitalism in general, regardless of the many country-specific distinctions that might be of great significance. The features of the socioeconomic framework that characterized Russia in the late 1990s can also be found in many "transitional" polities outside of the core of the contemporary world economy.

Accordingly, my forecast differed from that of forecasters who were essentially optimistic about the allegedly approaching completion of the transitional period and who envisioned a young and energetic Russian capitalism about to take the country's future into its mighty hands. For my part, I claimed that a transition from the state of affairs that had emerged in Russia's economy by that time to an economy like that which characterized developed countries was not going to be smooth or "natural." Rather, it was a rare historic opportunity that required persistent, intentional efforts by Russia's entire political class.

I reasoned that, in order to achieve this, Russia needed a new social contract and the establishment of fundamentally new institutions that would be used to implement genuine rather than fictitious reforms. Many of my critics dismissed this as tedious lecturing, as a justification for my alleged reluctance to assume responsibility for taking part in the transformation of Russia, which they viewed as perhaps complicated but, overall, "moving in the right direction."

In quite a few of my writings, I pointed out that the system of peripheral capitalism that was rapidly taking shape in Russia had an internal resource for survival and could sustain itself for decades without major changes, especially in the absence of external threats challenging its durability.[2] This system relied upon its own social base among those strata and groups in society that were able to extract bureaucratic and criminal rents from their current position, in spite of the volatility of the rules of the game—and that could sometimes bend those rules in their favor. Moreover, vast reserves of raw materials, first of all hydrocarbons, enabled the Kremlin not only to guarantee the long-term well-being of the privileged class (that is, those who could take advantage of their position in society to extract rents) but also to provide jobs and incomes to the fairly large strata of those who were able to capture, in one way or another, the flows of income and demand resulting from the extraction and the utilization of these natural resources. This kind of a system has a high probability of stabilizing itself for an extended period. Such a system, no matter how ugly and inefficient, has no rigid internal constraints that would impede its stabilization. Moreover, in the medium term it can coexist with economic growth, a rise in incomes and consumption, and a prevailing sense of increasing prosperity.

Accordingly, I believed that only politically driven, intentional actions, with the support of the majority of economic elites, would be able to pull Russia out of this ill-fated equilibrium of a stagnation-prone system. I saw as questionable the idea of a spontaneous evolution of the country's mind-set and institutions, which was touted by many back then. That was why I repeatedly called for a broad-based nongovernmental coalition of forces in support of reforms and, as a matter of fact, for imposing a new economic policy agenda upon the authorities. This agenda included the legitimation of state authority and property ownership in Russia through their broad-based recognition by the public, based on the principles of the rule of law, justice, and social responsibility as well as the inseparability of the rights and obligations of property owners. It required preventing the concentration of power in anyone's hands and the establishment of mechanisms for a legally impeccable replacement of those in power, through pressure from below. Finally, my agenda called for greater transparency in decision-making by government agencies, political parties, lobbying groups, and so on. As a means toward these goals, I proposed to develop a broad-based agreement to be signed by representatives of the government, big business, and civil society. Such an agreement would lay out a road map of practical actions toward these goals.[3]

Today, as I evaluate the course of events since the turn of the century, I do not see much change to the picture that I have outlined, or anything to indicate that the solutions I originally identified need much revision. Due to the growth in export revenues and their subsequent redistribution via market mechanisms and through the federal budget, Russia experienced, until 2008, an undeniably substantial increase in incomes and wealth. Yet this did not lead to changes in the essential characteristics of Russia's society.

Russia's capitalism was and remains a typical (while, at the same time, rather distinctive) example of the periphery of the world economy. It is economically as well as technologically dependent on its core, which is the developed countries of the West. It also has preserved vast enclaves of archaic economic and social ways of life and is devoid of internal engines of growth and development in the form of an autonomous accumulation of capital built on a technological foundation that would have the ability to renew itself.

Over these years, the structure of Russia's economy has not become more complex. To the contrary, it has come even closer to an economic model that is oriented toward external demand, a narrow circle of traditional products, and external sources of investment. Moreover, in the past few years the situation has become worse, in that labor-intensive sectors, such as construction and services, have become increasingly reliant upon the importation of a workforce from abroad (despite all the rhetoric to the contrary and even the administrative actions intended to curb this trend). Meanwhile, a large part of Russia's own human resources are being eroded through open and covert emigration of its youngest and most capable workers, along with the downward social drift of its able-bodied population in the economically disadvantaged and the so-called unpromising areas of the country.

Furthermore, as the years of the global military and ideological standoff between the Soviet Union and the United States recede further into the past, the perception of Russia—both by its own people and by the outside world—increasingly reflects its present condition. It holds the status of a weighty but peripheral and relatively insignificant part of the world economy. Its global role has been reduced to, on the one hand, supplying other countries with oil, gas, and some other raw materials, as well as the "mass consumption" products of its military industry and the provision of some transport services, and, on the other hand, the importation of foreign goods to satisfy domestic demand. While Russia's huge nuclear stockpiles certainly protect it from the threat of a direct foreign invasion, it cannot secure it an image of a highly developed country, capable of claiming a seat among global economic, technological—and, thus, political—leaders. The perception of Russia as the successor to the Soviet Union—a great power that had laid claim to technological leadership in at least a few key areas—has gradually morphed into the image of an economy that, while promising, is incomparably more humble in every sense, being in the same category as India and Brazil. In Russia, there has been a growing sense of a yawning gap between the developed world, primarily the countries of Europe, and their own country, which has gotten rid of the label of a "postsocialist" and "transitional" economy but has not succeeded in becoming a part of this developed world. Strictly speaking, this feeling has been one of the foremost reasons for the abrupt growth of anti-Western sentiments among Russia's elite during these years.

But the worst (though perhaps the most important) news is that—due to the peculiar character of the reforms implemented in the 1990s, and of privatization in particular—Russia did not produce a class of autonomous and socially responsible wealth owners capable of collectively assuming the role of the advocate, organizer, and driving force of active institutional transformation. Only such a transformation would have put an end to the spontaneous reproduction of the flawed and stagnation-inducing post-Soviet forms of economic organization. Of course, Russia does have a few entrepreneurs of this kind, but they ended up without a unifying, powerful, and effective organization, a suitable political consciousness, or even a sense of solidarity as a class. And without such a class, which would be endowed with financial, organizational, and political resources, the building of a broad-based coalition in support of the reforms becomes virtually hopeless. Meanwhile, in the absence of this kind of a pressure from below, the authorities behave as an indifferent spectator at best, and at worst are actively blocking any changes in the status quo that would be unfavorable to them, viewing such changes as a threat to their own political stability and to the perpetuation of their privileged status.

Thus, it is rather obvious that the issue of far-reaching institutional reforms has been effectively taken off Russia's political agenda—partly, and perhaps primarily, for the reason that I have outlined. This means, in turn, that Russia is now firmly trapped in its peripheral capitalism for the long haul.

This is essentially what led me to address in greater detail the flip side of this complex phenomenon, the political order of Russia's post-Soviet capitalism. I see at least three reasons for the need for a more attentive analysis of these political dynamics. As noted earlier, one distinctive feature of the system of peripheral capitalism is that its economy has no internal, autonomous incentives for its development. While it may grow under the impact of external demand for its goods and services, or because of favorable short-term trends in its economic environment, it is intrinsically incapable of developing toward higher complexity, of finding new venues and engines for its internal development. It is in a state of semi-stagnation and unilateral dependence upon the leading industrial nations. The prospects for overcoming this condition and for changing its position in the global economy, even if only in the long term, hinge entirely upon the intentionality of government policies, upon the authorities' political will and their readiness to undertake strenuous efforts in this direction and to incur personal risks and even sacrifices for the sake of achieving the goals that are important for society at large. This leads us to consider whether a political system should provide such incentives and such opportunities to its political class in the first place.

The second reason is that Russia's public consciousness is marked by the actual presence and even the domination of a plainly simplistic approach to the analysis of its political realities and their causes. In most of the debates, the issues are presented in an overly simplistic manner and contradictory developments are ignored. Meanwhile, the motivations and intents behind the actions of the key players are attributed to unsophisticated, a priori explanations rather than being determined through careful analysis. In this process, the widespread use of stereotypical jargon and abstract, quasi-scientific reasoning utterly detached from realities more often leads away from the substance of the issue rather than contributing to its understanding. Of course, having a grasp of the gist of the type of governance that has taken shape in Russia by now, and of the limits of its reach, is of paramount importance in assessing its prospects and the possibilities for its transformation.

The third and final reason that more attentive analysis is needed is the unpleasant fact that, at least in the past two decades, and perhaps over a longer period, the international community at large has been losing its sense of direction, principles, and purpose, while the search for new ones has so far not been terribly successful. Too much has changed in world affairs since the end of the Cold War, when the governments of leading Western countries acquired more freedom of action compared to the peak of the military and political standoff between the Soviet bloc and NATO. The formerly established goals and rules of behavior have lost their relevance, but defining new ones has become a protracted exercise and has led to acute disagreements among the once consolidated Western elites. Moreover, changes in the structure and the characteristics of Western economies, along with the spread of qualitatively new digital technologies in those countries, have substantially altered the functioning of their political systems (as shown, for example, by the financial and economic crisis of 2007–2009).

All of these changes have affected not just the group of countries known as the West but also their relationships with the rest—the nations on the periphery of global capitalism. To conceptualize the potential impact of these changes upon Russia and its position in the world, we need to get a better grasp of what Russia's political class is and how it relates to the political regime that has taken shape in the country. All of this constitutes the purpose of this book.

Let me make a few additional remarks of a general nature before moving on to this book's main argument. First of all, it is obvious that not everything in a given society is reducible to its economic foundations. While, at least in theory, Marxism leaned more toward economic determinism than any other school of thought, even Marxists allowed for considerable variations in the relation of the "political superstructure" to its "economic basis" (even though the meaning and the functionality of the superstructure in Marxism was extremely narrow and was reduced to servicing and sustaining the dominant property relationships in a given society).

As for the present-day notions of the political structure of society, they tend to posit merely indirect or the most general causal connection between the economic relationships and institutions prevalent in a given society and the principles and practices of its political governance. Thus, for example, there is a widespread assumption that economic competition has an inherent relationship to the existence of political competition in society, while economic rights and freedoms closely correlate with civil liberties and political freedoms and are guaranteed or preconditioned by them. It is also widely held that attributes of a political system such as universal voting rights and the separation of powers guarantee the free development of the markets and their mechanisms, while also counteracting excessive concentration of property ownership in the hands of the few and the emergence of monopolies. Finally, it is explicitly or implicitly accepted that competition always and everywhere leads to improved efficiency, both in the economy and in political governance.

Undoubtedly, at a sufficiently high level of abstraction, all these relationships apply. A great number of scholarly works establish these relationships with "scientific validity," using mathematical frameworks to perform analysis of carefully selected and suitably interpreted statistical data. Yet such causal relationships are more a matter of worldview and are largely theoretical. To assert that a classical market economy with a prevalence of private property ownership and a liberal political system of free and unregulated competition among ideas, citizens, and their associations are two sides of the same coin would be a stretch and would greatly oversimplify the tricky and at times less than fully rational configuration of societal relationships in real life.

The economic relations and the political system of a given society have an impact on each other, but in reality this impact is not so simple. First and foremost, it is never as rigid and unequivocal as some claim it to be. The causal relationships noted earlier are not deterministic but rather probabilistic; further, they can be found only across large samples of units of analysis, selected according to intentionally specified criteria. Thus, in spite of the efforts to prove the validity of these relationships with sophisticated math, they essentially remain hypothetical.

And they may very well prove to be false, if the set of data used for the analysis is selected and prepared in a different way or if an attempt is made to test them over a longer period of time.

In this regard, a lot depends upon the interpretation of the meaning and the functioning of specific institutions, and this interpretation, in turn, greatly depends upon the interpreters' interests and biases. This is even more the case when we deal with such intrinsically subjective notions as freedom or the lack thereof, democracy, legitimacy, and so on. Besides, political and economic institutions influence each other, and not necessarily in any one direction. Thus, economic factors may be objectively pushing political institutions to develop in a certain direction, but these institutions themselves may, for whatever reasons, be developing in the opposite direction, while exerting a pressure on the economy to place it in the framework of a different kind of relationship. Otherwise, we would not be observing such a wide variety of disparate and eclectic models of political governance as we see today, with the coexistence of heterogeneous principles and mechanisms that at times operate in mutually incompatible directions.

One way or another, in reality, the system of relationships in any given society is always complex and can never be precisely and adequately described with two or three commonplace labels or characterizations. Trivial as it may sound, life is indeed always richer, as the expression goes, than can be captured by any schematic representation. And the direction of the dynamics, let alone the long-term developmental trends, cannot be grasped or identified in the short term but only from a sufficient historical distance.

Going back to our discussion of Russia's capitalism in its post-Soviet "edition," it is notable that, even now, more than two decades since it began taking shape, the prospects of the further evolution of its political superstructure and of its capacity to ensure the country's economic and social development are still far from clear. It is true that a lot is now clearer than it used to be, especially in comparison to how things looked around the year 2000 or 2005. Some of the potential directions and opportunities available back then were not utilized. Many of them have entirely disappeared from the horizon, forever—or at least for a very long time. Others, to the contrary, have turned into the most plausible and even unavoidable scenario of Russia's prospective political development, which is going to mold and adjust the road map of Russia's potential options and developments at any given time. And yet the country's future is still not fully clear and is still indeterminate.

I certainly anticipate many objections to this statement. Critics will point out that, throughout the past decade, Russia's political institutions have evolved in a rather clear direction. Namely, genuine political competition has been increasingly curtailed; the checks and balances, to the extent and in the forms that they existed in Russia at the turn of the twenty-first century, have been eliminated; and the activities of political parties and of the legislature and the everyday implementation of the laws have degenerated, if viewed from the standpoint of the norms of parliamentary democracy and rule of law. Meanwhile, the authorities have been paying less and less attention to the opinions and the interests of the many different groups and strata of Russian society when passing new laws; the extent of subjective and arbitrary interpretation of legal norms and the selectivity of their implementation have been increasing; the role of the central authorities in regional decision-making has grown, while the extent of their ownership and control of several fields of economic activity, including mass media, has markedly increased; and the room for competition has noticeably shrunk—not only in politics and public affairs but also in many industries, first and foremost in the resource industries and in export-oriented businesses.

Indeed, the past ten to fifteen years saw many changes in this direction, occurring with different degrees of intensity. I will be discussing them repeatedly in the rest of the book. And yet I believe it would be wrong to portray the turn of the century as a critical turning point, when these trends allegedly supplanted something entirely opposite that had prevailed in the course of the preceding decade.

It is true that the 1990s were indeed characterized by deeper contradictions and the fragmentation within the power elite as well as by the absence of a cohesive, dominant group tightly knit together through rigid internal discipline. It is also true that Boris Yeltsin, Russia's chief executive at the time, relied—had to rely—to a greater extent upon political maneuvering among various interest groups. This created an illusion of a genuine political pluralism, not only in public life but also in the process of determining government policies in a wide range of areas.

Nevertheless, it would be disingenuous, if not outright shameless, to present the 1990s in Russia as a time of the blossoming of parliamentary government, under which the next team of key officeholders is determined through elections whose outcome has not been fixed in advance. Back then, just as in today's Russia, the composition of these teams was decided by the arbitrary will of one man who had been brought by the course of events (and to a large extent by happenstance) to the top of the government hierarchy. And just as in today's Russia, the correlation of power among different groups and factions within the system of government had nothing to do with the results of an election. Instead, it reflected the personal considerations and calculations of that sole individual—Boris Yeltsin—taking into account objectively available opportunities as well as risks. And when one speaks of the "antidemocratic" trends in the first decade of this century, we must keep in mind that these trends did not reflect some kind of a metamorphosis of the political machine and of the elite that was using it. Rather, it represented the ongoing consolidation and simplification of this elite in response to the government's offer of less disruptive and historically more familiar foundations and frameworks for its functioning.

In other words, for Russia, the turn of the twenty-first century was no turning point. There was no switch from one set of principles and one system of governance to a different one. What happened around the year 2000, instead, was that the system of rule that had already taken shape by then had become structured and, in its own way, accomplished, having acquired a clear internal logic for its functioning, and then transitioned into a new stage of its existence. This was the stage of the system's greater maturity and, so to speak, overtness. At this new stage, the basic principles of the organization of governance became fully expressed in accordance with the logic of those principles, in the relatively undisguised form of the institutions of a more fiercely authoritarian state, operating in a capitalist environment but on the periphery of the global capitalist system. To put it differently, the past two decades of Russia's socioeconomic and political development produced a system that is by and large reflective of the characteristics and the global role of Russia's peripheral capitalism. This is what I call a political system of peripheral authoritarianism, and it has had adverse consequences for Russia to this day.

2

RUSSIA TODAY

The History of How and Why It Came to Be

DEFINING THE POLITICAL FRAMEWORK OF RUSSIA'S CAPITALISM

My take on the political system of present-day Russia is that it is an authoritarian country of a peripheral, or marginal, type. Let me clarify: for me, this characterization is not a means to denounce the country or to slap Russia's government with a negative, op-ed-style label. I see it as first and foremost an accurate and unbiased assessment of the realities of today's Russia. Such an assessment is not intended to give rise to emotions and value judgments. Each of us lives within a certain frame of reference, a sociopolitical environment that we need to comprehend in order to take advantage of it, rather than ignoring it as a priori defective.

This is not to say that we ought to eliminate our personal bias toward such a system and simply accept today's Russia. To the contrary, I continue to think that a thorough political reform would be in Russia's interest as well. The kind of reform that I envision here would lead to the following outcomes:

- altering the principles upon which Russia's institutions of government are currently formed;

- establishing a governance structure that would include, perhaps for the first time in Russia's history, a significant element of political competition and the devolution of power;
- transferring a significant part of the resources controlled by the authorities from the present single center of power in the Kremlin to various lower layers and to other branches of government; and
- affirming the requirement for a regular alternation of political forces in government, as well as creating a mechanism of overall accountability of all government institutions to each other and of responsibility for any violation of established procedures.

Clearly, such a reform would imply a comprehensive dismantling of the relations of authority that are currently in place, even though it would not involve revolutionary upheavals and a breakdown of the institutions of government as such.

Nevertheless, I believe it is more appropriate first to gain a clear and precise understanding of how Russia's machinery of governance works today, to trace the path of its formation, and to make sense of the mechanisms that are currently in place. We need this knowledge as the basis for steering the course of events in the country at least to safety, if not in the ideal desirable direction. And for this we need to address our recent history, beginning first and foremost with the developments of the first decade of the twenty-first century, which was also the first decade of Vladimir Putin's rule.

As I mentioned earlier, I do not view the year 2000, when Putin was elected to Russia's presidency for the first time—or, as many others do, the first years of his term (2002 or 2003)—as a watershed moment. It was not really a turnaround of any kind that changed the direction of the development of Russia's political system from a putatively democratic track toward something opposite, toward the dismantling of the institutions of democracy and the restricting of political freedoms in every possible way. To the contrary, I believe that the entire period since the collapse of the Soviet state has seen a continuous consolidation of the authoritarian power of the bureaucracy, operating under the distinctive conditions of Russia's peripheral capitalism. But, to substantiate this argument, we first need to sort out the terminology and the notions behind it, as is necessary for a truly meaningful analysis of any political system.

Before turning to terminology, let me add a few caveats that will put subsequent discussion on a more solid ground. First, any discussion about the substance and the logic inherent in an existing political system inevitably involves simplifications; in real life, some features and manifestations of such a system will never fit into any analytical model. Such a model, while helpful in understanding the essential features of a system and the directions of potential changes within it, can never grasp it in its totality.

Thus, for example, any textbook on the theory of state governance will contain references to a range of theoretical models—from the natural or social contract to Mancur Olson's model of government as either a "stationary" or a "roving" bandit.[1] But no academic in their right mind would think of using these models as exhaustive explanations of real-life political developments. Life is always more complicated than any model or theory; people involved in politics are rather diverse and are motivated by a wide variety of factors. Political decisions are overwhelmingly a product of compromise, both overt and implicit, and their implementation in practice is always very different from the decision-makers' intent. Thus, my discussion of Russia's political system is merely an attempt to grasp and to explain its overall logic, to stubbornly run through myriad deviations from it and through a large number of disconnected events and phenomena.

Our second but no less important caveat is that the notions used to describe a system's overall logic not only are subject to individual interpretations affected by personal biases but also change over time. We should always keep this in mind. Any particular term may mean vastly different things in different historical periods. As a result, some seemingly fundamental disagreements over specific political events may be caused by merely a difference in the understanding of certain emotionally charged terms, while being completely insubstantial in practice. This applies first and foremost to such notions as democracy, equality, public good, and the like. Some of the seemingly scientific terms with a broad consensus about their usage are routinely subjected to wide-ranging interpretations that disrupt all prior consensus around them.

With these caveats in mind, let me also note the following about the terminology used. First of all, the term "democratic," widely used by intellectuals to characterize political systems and developments, should actually be applied with a great degree of caution. It is too abstract when used generically and too subjectively biased and vague when used in specific contexts. It is used more to differentiate oneself from the "other" than to denote a sum total of specific characteristics or political tools.

As we know from history, neither universal voting nor the existence of political parties nor the absence of criminal prosecution for political speech or for a criticism of the authorities—in sum, no single mechanism among those currently identified by mainstream Western intellectuals as being "democratic"—can be assumed to be a universally applicable, characteristic feature of democracy or its defining element. Moreover, even when taken together, these elements can produce political systems that are fundamentally dissimilar in spirit and in the direction of their development. Thus, the division of countries into "democratic" and "undemocratic" still ends up being colored by one's personal bias toward identifying with the "good guys," as opposed to the "bad" and the "other."

It is more meaningful to characterize political systems on the basis of a different pair of notions: that of a competition-based system, in which political groups openly vie for power against each other within a set of mutual restraints, versus an authoritarian system, in which power is not acquired within the legal framework of an open political competition. In a competition-based system, power is distributed, one way or another, among different centers of authority that most often serve as alternatives to each other; in the authoritarian case, one leader or a group organized along corporate lines single-handedly has a grip upon the exercise of power.

Accordingly, the mechanisms of transferring power from one group to another are different in each case. In a competition-oriented system, power is transferred through an electoral process whose legitimacy is recognized by all participant groups but is not single-handedly controlled by any one of them. Meanwhile, in an authoritarian system, power is transferred by an arbitrary decision of the ruling group or its leader on the basis of specific power relationships. Under this scenario, the particular manner in which the power gets transferred is not all that important. Under an authoritarian system, power can be transferred either by a simple appointment, by a top-down restructuring or reforming of the machinery of governance, or through general elections, provided that the outcome can be engineered in advance. Under a competitive system, there can be a wide variety of specific electoral systems, with dozens or even hundreds of different arrangements, whereby officials may be elected directly, indirectly, or in a multiple-stage process, and with different sets of both voters and candidates. In a competitive system, even the number and the character of restrictions on the electoral process is not critically important.

What is most important is that the system must provide an opportunity to remove a ruling team or group from power, in a transparent and institutionally determined manner, so that the rulers cannot establish the length of their own terms in power and cannot predetermine their successors. In other words, the system must guarantee that any group of rulers will have no choice but to step down, without an opportunity to name a successor whose ascent to power it would be able to secure.

Naturally, the prerequisite for such a system is that no single group has an effective grip on power and that power is spread out among at least two or three or more groups, each wielding the requisite legal tools of organized coercion. Accordingly, the primary characteristic of a competition-based political system is that no single individual or group of people has full power and no one can issue decisions without considering how other groups and political forces will respond to them. Most importantly, such a system has embedded safeguards against any attempt to usurp power in the country. In other words, any individual or group of people having access to the levers of power are fully aware that their attempt to cross the boundaries of their authority will immediately trigger the mechanisms whose end result will be the use of legally organized coercion to push them back to where they belong.

We can agree to call a competitive political system "democratic," as many often do. Yet, at the same time, we must keep in mind that, in this context, the term "democracy" is related to its original Greek meaning—"people's power"—in approximately the same manner as economic agents in real life relate to the ideal *homo economicus* from classical economic theory—an imaginary human being from a textbook, which has no personification in reality. In other words, we can use the term "democratic" as long as we realize that its factual meaning in this case has little in common with its formal definition.

In any case, "democracy" here does not mean "people's power" or "power for the people" or even "power in the interests of the people." Rather, it is simply a characterization of a political arrangement under which power is not concentrated in the hands of any one elite group but instead is distributed among several groups in accordance with specific rules that secure an alternation of different groups in government. It is also a system that relies upon compromise among these groups, rather than everybody's subordination to the will and the interests of a single dominant group. Either way, at present, competitive and authoritarian systems of governance exist in about equal numbers in the world around us. It seems that no one has yet been able to come up with a formula explaining the emergence of a particular system and its occasional transformation into its opposite—at least not in a clear and compelling way.

This is not to say that there are no theories about it; there are plenty. Moreover, the spontaneously developed and informal community of professional economists and political scientists has formulated (and named after themselves) a variety of hypotheses on this subject, by going through virtually every conceivable relationship between types of political systems and such factors as the level of income and wealth, the rates and quality of economic growth, the stages of an economic cycle, and so on.[2] However, every such hypothesis is met with a counterhypothesis. Meanwhile, the general issue of what comes first—democracy or economic growth—has long since been elevated to such theoretical heights that any attempts to apply it to derive real-life conclusions are hardly ever taken seriously by anyone any longer.

Moreover, in some instances, boundaries between competition-based and authoritarian systems of governance are getting blurred. At least one reason for this is the existence of a considerable number of borderline cases, in which no particular group has a clear-cut, single-handed grip on all resources of power across the board and yet the ruling group enjoys such a significant advantage in the distribution of these resources that, in reality, competing groups are not able to apply effective checks and balances on its power. In such instances, the classification of a given system as either competition-based or authoritarian may depend upon the judgment and the personal bias of an individual observer. In addition, because the situation within a given system may fluctuate rapidly, the exact moment of its transition from a competitive to an authoritarian state or vice versa, from one logic of its functioning to another, may be hard to identify and to capture.

Finally, anyone who seeks to get an unbiased grasp of a given situation and to think seriously should, at the very least, be put on guard by peremptory judgments and emotionally colored labels (such as "dictatorship" or "tyranny") as well as by sweeping historical comparisons. Attempts to hide oneself behind sweeping characterizations are most often used to conceal the lack of information and knowledge about the circumstances. As noted in Oscar Wilde's *The Importance of Being Earnest*, "The truth is rarely pure and never simple." Needless to say, this does not mean that people should not take their stands as citizens or pass value judgments; yet every development and every phenomenon need to be viewed holistically, with all their nuances, contradictions, and complexities.

Another characteristic of political systems that I want to emphasize here is their relationship to such concepts as the public good and societal goals. This is by no means of secondary importance. There is a prevailing view, both among the general public and among authoritative analysts of sociopolitical systems, that the classification of a political system as either competition-based ("democratic") or authoritarian has no strict relationship to any societal goals that may be pursued by such a system and that may be connected, one way or another, to the notion of public good (such as, for example, acceleration of economic growth, technological and social modernization of the country, and the like).

On the one hand, history provides us with a plenty of examples of political systems under which the freedom of political activities—roughly, competitive elections and alternation of political leaders and parties in power (at times, very frequent alternation), to say nothing of freedom of speech and of the media—coexisted with pervasive corruption, total indifference of the authorities to societal needs, and the decline of order, morale, and public safety. The United States at the start of the twentieth century is perhaps the best example of this. In the post–World War II period, competitive political systems proved to be no panacea against corruption and inefficiency, either in developed countries such as Italy or in the developing world, as, for example, in India and Brazil.

The opposite is also true: there are examples of successful authoritarian modernizations, such as in Singapore, Turkey, South Korea, and, to a certain extent, Japan, where power continuously resided in the hands of a de facto single political force throughout the periods of their high-speed economic growth, while other, less influential political groups were denigrated and denounced. Mainland China and, possibly, Vietnam are the latest examples of countries that are widely viewed as having, at least to some extent, successfully modernized while being under an unquestionably authoritarian political system.

The mainstream of political thinking in Western societies generally views the possibility of accelerated economic growth and modernization under an authoritarian regime as an option applicable only to those countries that have fallen behind in their economic, technological, and social development, and only within a brief historical period of their "catching up" with the West, when their medium-term goals are rather obvious and can be relatively easily articulated in formal terms, becoming the political goals of an authoritarian state.[3] This may very well be true; yet, even with these caveats, we still have to face the actual discrepancy, present over fairly long historical periods, between, on the one hand, the characteristics of a political regime in terms of its internal competitiveness and, on the other, the extent to which it can effectively accomplish large-scale national objectives.

Furthermore, some eminent thinkers, such as, for example, economist Robert Aumann, who won the Nobel Prize in 2005, believe that the longer time horizons enjoyed by authoritarian regimes enable them to achieve the goals of modernization more easily—provided, of course, that they are not corrupted by their lack of accountability and control over their power. Daron Acemoglu and James Robinson, whose works are frequently referred to, claim that the threat of a revolution may compel elites under authoritarian systems to restrain their appetites, to be more rational in their expenses, and to provide larger amounts of public goods.[4]

But, of course, all the ruminations of this kind merely reflect one's theoretical assumptions; if they can be put to any practical use, it is only to a very limited extent. It is certainly clear that there is no uniform linkage of any kind between the form of government and the motivations of the rulers and that if the ruling group has any motivation whatsoever to modernize the country, such motivation is typically mostly related to the overall attitudes of the political and economic elites and to the personal characteristics of their most active members. It is equally clear that these elites' intent to modernize is conditioned, to a large extent, by the country's prior history in its entirety as well as by the characteristics of the structure of its economy, the extent of its participation in the world economic system and international political institutions, and so forth.

All this will be applied in more detail to the case of Russia in other parts of this book. In the meantime, let me note as a matter of fact that a goal-oriented design of any political system, organized with a view toward the pursuit of the goals related to economic growth and modernization, is a feature that stands altogether apart and must be analyzed on its own.

A final issue worth mentioning here, in relation to the widespread classification of political systems and the terminology attached to it, is about the character of the equilibrium in a political system and the direction in which any such model or system may be developing. Setting aside for the time being the causes of and the driving forces that define the direction of development of a given political system, let us note that a political system may be either dynamic or static. If its specific elements are changing to adapt to life's demands, if they help to remove the barriers that have emerged on the path of the development of society, if they form the requisite new institutions in response to societal demands, then it is a dynamic system. However, if within its framework there are forces and mechanisms that basically work to forestall changes within the system, to extinguish every external attempt to introduce change and instead to keep bringing the system back to an equilibrium of stagnation, then such a system tends to stagnate and to suppress change.

The systems of the first, dynamic type are, virtually by definition, capable of reforming themselves in an evolutionary manner. This enables them to prevent, for relatively long periods of time, major societal upheavals and associated shocks. Most often, these are the kinds of regimes that, even if perhaps authoritarian, do not neglect the need for a dialogue and pursuit of workable compromise solutions in order to reconcile divergent interests and approaches within the political class. While the separation of powers and the institutions of parliamentary democracy are the most efficient tools for achieving such a compromise, they are not the only such instrument, and they are not irreplaceable.

Political systems of the second type, which are stagnation-prone or demodernizing, inevitably result in explosive social and political disturbances of a revolutionary type. Such political systems may provide an appearance—or, rather, an illusion—of stability for a relatively short time, yet they are unable to provide resolution to emerging tensions. Instead, these tensions keep piling up until their scale is practically no longer compatible with the regular functioning of the system's institutions. At that point, they lead to a serious political crisis. The system may be able to postpone a resolution for the time being by treating the symptoms of the problem, either by populist campaigns or by suppressing dissent. If, however, this is not feasible, then the resolution of this crisis leads, in the best case, to the collapse of the political system and its replacement with a new one that is more fitted to the requirements of the moment. Or, in the worst case, the entire statehood in its prior form may collapse, in which case the new institutions of governance will have to be built from scratch, or even from a lower starting point.

The characteristics used in this classification of political systems also do not have any strict and uniform relationship with the extent to which a given system is either competition-based or authoritarian. In a specific situation at a given point in time, "democratic" models of political governance may turn out to be unable to meet the current challenges. And by not providing society with the means to initiate a radical (or seemingly radical) transformation, a democratic system may end up contributing to the development of a deep political crisis with long-term repercussions. To name just a few historical examples, this is what happened in Weimar Germany, in Chile and Argentina in the mid-1970s, and to some extent in present-day Greece, which has bogged down in a quagmire of multiple internal divisions and economic challenges.

Granted, authoritarian regimes are more often prone to failures of governance, and one could cite plenty of examples in Africa and in Latin America. And as a rule, such failed regimes tend to be replaced with other regimes of the same authoritarian type. Some of these new regimes manage to achieve impressive gains in the quality of governance and to tackle, at least in part, the problems that led to the crisis, but others turn out to be just as powerless as their predecessors, and it is just a matter of time before they go down as well.

Nevertheless, there are also examples of a different kind—regimes built along an authoritarian model yet managing to go, without much pain, through necessary changes that provide them with more flexibility, adaptability, and sophistication in their means of control. Not always, but in some of these cases, such changes results in a gradual "democratization," that is, the expansion of the role of representative institutions; the erosion of the ruling group's monopolistic control over the resources of governance, including its control over the institutions of coercion; the increase of the autonomy and the power of the judiciary; and the end to the use of law enforcement agencies for partisan political purposes. Such developments could be observed, for example, in Spain at the end of Francisco Franco's rule, as well as in South Korea and several other autocracies in Asia. But, of course, there have been also examples of an opposite development—the decay of representative institutions and the transformation of competition-based political systems into authoritarian regimes of varying degrees of severity.

RUSSIA IN THE 1990S: THE "GOLDEN AGE" OF REFORMS?

Taking into account all that I have said thus far, let me start with an overview of Russia in the 1990s. It was then, in the wake of the abrupt collapse of Soviet statehood, and on the shaky ground of dysfunctional institutions and complete disorientation in the minds of Russia's legislators and its law enforcement powers, that the political system of today's Russia began taking shape.

Those who have forgotten those first post-Soviet years, or who were too young at the time to remember them, should be aware that the political system of the new Russia, as it was emerging on paper in 1991–1992, had no future from the outset. This was so even if we set aside the issue of how much of the actual control over the situation in the country was in the hands of Russia's new authorities and even if we assume that the formally existing institutions were actually functioning and shaping the real situation in the country.

What looked, in the late 1980s, like the awakening of democracy (i.e., the establishment, one after another, of new institutions that appeared to be taking over the functions of deliberation and decision-making) did have its positive impact as a peaceful revolution of sorts. And yet, in the long term, it was not at all universally positive. The situation was rapidly becoming fraught with many legal and institutional conflicts, while a few of its important procedural aspects, related to the mechanisms of making and implementing decisions and of controlling their implementation, were rather vague.

It would take several pages to draw a list of all these conflicts and uncertainties. Let me mention just a few of them here. The Congress of People's Deputies, Russia's legislature at the time, had an ambiguous status as the highest authority in the country, with no institutional tools to exercise this authority. President Boris Yeltsin, on the other hand, was in control of virtually every practical policy tool, though he was legally constrained by the legislature, which could formally impose on him particular policies while bearing no responsibility for their feasibility. It was largely this ambiguity that, in 1993, resulted in the situation in which the legislature's showdown with Yeltsin and his government over the president's right to dissolve the legislature and hold fresh elections went beyond the framework of legally established procedures and put the country on the brink of a large-scale armed internal conflict. Moreover, within the government, the boundaries between the process of legislating and that of governing were extremely blurred, which led, at times, to complete uncertainty for the lower layers of the executive administration, for the judiciary, and for the armed agencies of the government.

In addition, the conspicuous weakness of the judiciary system and the lack of effective instruments for the implementation of its decisions resulted in virtually limitless opportunities for all kinds of power abuse, while making it impossible to use the courts as the adjudicator of disputes or as a disciplining power. It was already then, in 1992–1993, that the ruling circle began cultivating and encouraging an attitude of disregard for the law while replacing universally applicable, long-term, and legally binding norms with personalized, ad hoc, and temporary arrangements between government authorities and economic agents. The withdrawal of law enforcement agencies from the activities necessary to ensure compliance with business deals and contracts, along with the uncertainty about the rules of behavior that would ensure normal economic activities, complicated matters even more.

Finally, enormous uncertainty was caused by the de jure dissolution of the Soviet Union while retaining de facto, for a certain period of time and without any special agreements about it, a shared currency, a shared customs control, and a jointly managed transportation and energy infrastructure.[5] In turn, the lack of clarity about the legal basis for managing these shared systems led to the same preponderance of individual, personalized deal-making over legal norms and to a misperception of democracy as the freedom of will exercised in the absence of appropriately established, stable, and universally applicable rules and procedures.

Even this incomplete list of issues shows that the political formation spontaneously emerging out of the breakdown of the Soviet system of governance had no central organizing principle and would not be able to stabilize itself either in the short term or in the long term. To gain at least some relative stability, it had to evolve, one way or another. Only through change could it transcend its most acute contradictions and acquire some routines that would help to prevent wild, unpredictable swings from one side to another. And, essentially, this evolution constitutes the gist of the first stage of Russia's post-Soviet political history, comprising most of the 1990s.

The first and arguably the most important choice that had to be made during this historically important period was the choice between a competition-based and an authoritarian political system. I believe that this choice was more or less completed with the adoption of Russia's new constitution, between October and December 1993, and then finalized on the eve of and during the presidential election of 1996, when Yeltsin was reelected, and in its aftermath. Those years made it clear that, even though political pluralism was being preserved and there were at least a few groups within the elite, each represented by a team of political players, the instruments of political power actually were not divided and distributed among these groups to even a minimally necessary extent. Without such a distribution of power resources, mutual checks and balances cannot function.

The degree of concentration of resources in the hands of the dominant elite group that coalesced around the presidential staff of Boris Yeltsin was sufficient to enable it to manipulate all other groups and to prevent them from getting an opportunity to assert any practical influence upon government, let alone to be able to replace it in the Kremlin. After some serious hesitation, this ruling group finally decided to hold the presidential elections in 1996, and, formally speaking, this implied the possibility of a nonviolent but still involuntary replacement of this group of people in power. Yet, in spite of this decision, there was only one election outcome that the ruling group deemed acceptable: the victory of Boris Yeltsin. And they secured this outcome with the highest degree of certainty, by using every kind of power resources that they had at their disposal.

Needless to say, those who now, for whatever reason, present the 1990s as a period of unprecedented blooming of democracy in Russia (in a positive value–laden sense of this term) tend to omit the fact that no one within Russia's ruling circle at the time accepted the possibility of voluntarily relinquishing power to another group of people on the basis of its winning more votes than were going to be won by Boris Yeltsin.

When running for Russia's presidency in the 1996 election, I saw this attitude of the ruling circle and took it into account. My goal was to bring substantial modifications to Russia's policies. I saw the purpose of my campaign as stopping the formation of an oligarchical system based upon the fusion of private business, property control, and political power, as well as standing up against corruption and the war in the North Caucasus. I was going to do it by offering an alternative to Boris Yeltsin's semicriminal economic policies, including his fraudulent loans-for-shares auctions, which handed large numbers of shares in Russia's major companies to a few well-connected banks in exchange for their loans to the government.

On this basis, I intended to come in third in the race (after Yeltsin and the Communist candidate, Gennady Zyuganov). Then I was going to put forward the condition for my support for Yeltsin in the runoff, namely, my appointment as prime minister, with the goal of introducing significant changes in economic and personnel policies. This was the only realistic chance to modify Yeltsin's course of action in politics and in the economy. But this opportunity was blocked by the oligarchical group of Anatoly Chubais and Boris Berezovsky. They did this by pumping up the media and pouring financial resources into the presidential campaign of General Alexander Lebed, making sure that he ended up with the third-highest number of votes and then, almost immediately after the election, destroying him as a politically significant player.

Of course, it is hard to tell which methods would have been used by Russia's ruling circle had it not been able to secure the outcome that was acceptable to it by employing the resources they had used already. In fact, neither is it fully clear which resources they did in fact use, and to what extent, to ensure the predictability of the outcome. This is not quite clear even today, nearly twenty years after those elections—the first-ever Russian elections that, in theory, could have sealed the fate of the ruling circle. From time to time, key protagonists of that period have hinted at the existence of some mysteries or, at the very least, something that has not been fully spelled out with regard to the run-up to the election and the contingency plans that were made for the eventuality that the election did not go their way. Regardless, I am sure that the ruling circle did not view the possibility of transferring power to another group, based on the outcome of those elections, as something realistic. Thus, already at this point, the first and foremost feature of an authoritarian political system took shape: the impossibility that the efforts of those outside of the dominant group could replace one group in power with a different group "from below," in a peaceful and legitimate fashion.

Let me reiterate: this does not mean that such a power transition is precluded on paper. A great many authoritarian regimes hold periodic elections for various levels of government so that, in theory, the possibility of an opposition victory in those elections cannot be ruled out. Yet, as long as a group of people ensconced at the height of power (most often united around an actual or an ex officio leader) has monopolized control over administrative power and over armed agencies, such a group has the real power to eliminate the probability of being ousted. Under such circumstances, even if an opposition gains the support of the majority of voters, this never leads to an official admission of defeat by the incumbent rulers nor to any practical implications in terms of a transfer of power.

But even such a scenario—an authoritarian incumbent losing the formal support of the majority of the country's population—is possible only as a result of very powerful pressures by forces and circumstances both internal and external to the system. Under regular conditions, most of society, especially its politically inactive segments, tend to provide the requisite support for the powers that be and their mode of governing, even if their exposure to the propagandistic and administrative machinery is minimal.

This is how it works in similar cases around the world. Strictly speaking, the pivotal—even, one might say, totemic—status of the liberal competition-based model of political system, in the mind-set of global elites and in the relevant scholarly or quasi-scholarly writings, is more a consequence of the financial and technological might of the group of countries that use this model, such as the United States and the United Kingdom, than of its successful spread in the larger world. It is often lost on many that the majority of our planet's population today lives in countries under authoritarian systems of rule, who differ among themselves in their ferocity in suppressing dissent, in their effectiveness, and in their political capabilities. Contrary to popular belief, such systems often do not assume the most extreme forms of bloody tyranny or practice total control over the life of their society. In more than a few cases, an authoritarian system does not preclude the population under its rule from enjoying a more or less unrestrained private life—as long as people are depoliticized. Even if this private life is quite removed from the ideals of efficiency and diversity, even if it is squeezed by an excess of arbitrary regulations and in some cases by ideological myths, nevertheless it is a relatively peaceful and stable life, with some space (however limited) for self-fulfillment in terms of personal aspirations and abilities.

It was precisely this kind of authoritarian system that took shape, in its basics, in the 1990s in Russia. The presidential election of 1996 still contained within it some chance, though not a very plausible chance, for the country to swerve onto a different trajectory, with the prospect of transitioning to a liberal, competition-based political system. In comparison, during the 1996–1999 period, the probability of moving to a different path at this particular turn of the spiral of Russia's history decreased to a statistically negligible level. At the present stage, for such a change of direction to happen, Russia would need to go through a period of a very serious reconceptualization that could lay the groundwork for another U-turn in its history.

Meanwhile, we should also revisit certain key events of Russia's development in the 1990s, which people tend to remember rarely and with which some are unfamiliar. First, the hyperinflation of 1992, which resulted from the liberalization of prices under total government ownership of economic property, created a supermonopolistic economic structure in Russia. This hyperinflation led to the expropriation of nearly 100 percent of individual savings, rapidly bringing the country's population to total misery.

Second, in 1993, President Yeltsin used force to resolve the confrontation between himself and the legislature (the Supreme Soviet). Subsequently, this resulted in the basically forcible integration into the new political system of a significant number of nationalists and so-called leftists. This was followed by the adoption, without debate and by dubious means, of a constitution that was authoritarian in its essence and in its logic.

Next, the war of 1994 in Chechnya led to many thousands of deaths and destroyed whatever modicum of positive legacy still remained from the Soviet era on the level of social psychology—that is, the remaining widespread norms of interethnic acceptance, at least in terms of outward behavior. That war consolidated the militaristic element in the ruling *nomenklatura*. It also damaged Russia's international reputation, while forcing many people in the outside world to ponder yet again the possibility of a military threat emanating from Moscow and to draw up plans for new dividing lines on the map of Europe.

The following year saw the launch of the fraudulent "privatization," which essentially amounted to the transfer of the economically most important government properties to a tiny circle of individuals with access to the authorities, virtually free of charge, via the so-called loans-for-shares auctions. This process laid the basis for the lack of legitimacy of private property ownership in Russia, contributed to the fusion between government officeholders and private property owners, and annihilated all autonomous sources for the funding of civil society initiatives.

The 1996 election, as I have stated, was another crucial turning point. Boris Yeltsin, the candidate of the ruling circle in the 1996 presidential election, was aggressively promoted to everybody else in Russia as "our" candidate, along the lines of the dictum "Everyone who is not with us is against us." After the election, through the distribution of plum portions of national economic wealth, free of charge, authorities continued to issue rewards to big business for their political service. This distribution of assets created an unbreakable bond between the country's political leadership and its new bourgeoisie. This was also the beginning of the doling out of government positions in exchange for one's personal services and as an expected source of the prospective officeholder's personal enrichment. Further, authorities persistently made an effort to tie one's patriotic feelings to the notion of being in the personal service of the chief of state (something that was noted by a classic Russian author of the nineteenth century, Mikhail Saltykov-Shchedrin, as the habit of confusing two notions: "Fatherland" and "Your Excellency").

It is also very important to note the emergence of a panic in the Kremlin about the possible fracturing of the elites into two competing groups within the dominant circle; this fear prompted the authorities to put a stranglehold on the political alternative that was coalescing at the time around Moscow mayor Yuri Luzhkov and former prime minister Yevgeny Primakov. The final stage in this process was the establishment of an institutionalized "successor to the president," when outgoing president Boris Yeltsin publicly announced Vladimir Putin as the sole candidate put forward by the ruling group to succeed him and provided him with all the resources and opportunities of incumbency that were controlled by that group.

As a matter of fact, this final move signaled the definitive installation in Russia of the second of the key features of an authoritarian system: the transfer of power by means of personalized succession, without a public competition for that role in any shape or form. In other words, this feature eliminates the ruling group's uncertainty about not only the electoral process but also the process of succession caused by individual biological reasons, such as the death or infirmity of the ruler. Let us note that even though this succession was initiated by the ruling circle and driven by the personal considerations of its members (some of whom later found that they had miscalculated), it happened with at least a tacit approval of society at large. The presence of electoral institutions, the freedom of political organizing and speech, did not preclude society as a whole, and especially its political class, from taking it as a given that, starting from the late 1990s, the ruling circle did not consider it necessary and would not allow its power and the personal fate of its members to depend upon the actual results of an uncontrolled popular vote at the general elections.

Of course, the attitude of the general public was not the only or even the most important factor. It became evident around the same time that the process of post-Soviet transformation did not produce the institutions capable of acting as independent branches of power and of ensuring the implementation of their decisions if those decisions were at odds with the interests or the wishes of the ruling circle. The representative bodies of government and the judiciary failed to gain the support necessary to become real counterweights to the executive agencies or to the informal, semicriminal, and even fully criminal quasi corporations that were spontaneously growing up around the executive and relying upon the machinery of violence. Even then, the much-touted "formation of the state of law and order" turned out to be, at best, wishful thinking and, at worst, a hypocritical cover-up of a de facto recognition of "might is right" as a formative instrument of governance.

Therefore, no candidate vying for power independently of the ruling circle had even minimally functional institutions to rely upon. For such candidates, the only means to gain a solid footing would be to construct their own organized entities endowed with administrative and coercive power resources, but this course of action presented risks for Russia's ruling party, and it was rejected by every responsible politician and public figure. Under those conditions, the country essentially faced a choice between the bad and the ugly, because a choice in favor of a political competition that would rely upon extralegal use of force would be essentially tantamount to choosing a state of civil war, even if it was not a full-blown civil war. And this, in turn, would have led to even more detrimental consequences than what we have before us today.

Admittedly, there are those who believe that, since the political system of the 1990s did not have such a high concentration of coercive, uniformed power as its fulcrum, it was therefore less centrally controlled and thus more democratic than its later variety was going to look, in 2005 or in 2010. Given that this opinion is rather popular among the liberal intelligentsia in Russia, let me comment upon this view.

It is an accurate observation inasmuch as it refers to the overall lack of governability as a feature of the socioeconomic situation at the time. However, as a matter of principle, no effective competition-based system can be built upon the loss of governability. The power wielded by warlords in confrontation with one another is a poor substitute for a competition among political teams that include more or less competent managers qualified to operate complicated government machinery. The diversity of political forces, also known as pluralism, implies a prevalence of democratic values in politics only in the presence of certain additional requirements.

The first of these requirements is the existence of relatively functional institutions in the country, which can transform such political diversity or pluralism from an end in itself into a force that makes institutions work in a more orderly fashion and increases officeholders' accountability for developments in the country. If such institutions do not exist, as they didn't exist in Russia in the late 1990s and don't exist today, then it makes no sense to lament the "abduction" of democracy after the year 2000. What then remains of that claim about a "democratic government of Yeltsin's liberal reformers" is merely the fact that, in the 1990s, the individuals in and around the Kremlin were closer to the Soviet-era liberal intelligentsia in terms of its political culture, ideology, and myths than were the group of people that took their place in the first decade of the twenty-first century. Nevertheless, if we pursue unbiased, dispassionate analysis of those two periods, it is obvious to me that the 1990s were merely an earlier, embryonic stage of the very same peripheral authoritarianism, a system that matured over the subsequent decade and a half. (Further justification for the use of the term "peripheral" in this context will be provided later in the book.)

Going back to the question of why Russia's political system developed along the path that it did in the 1990s, let me mention several explanatory factors. These factors made the potential formation of a competition-based model of the "Western" type an extremely complicated and therefore unlikely possibility. First and foremost, in Russia in the 1990s—and most consequentially in the early 1990s—there was no consensus among the elites about the most general, most fundamental rules and propositions around which the prospective political and economic system of the "new" Russia was going to be formed. And the presence of such a consensus is the key prerequisite in the formation of a functioning political system based upon competition among political forces. The fundamental issues on the public agenda at the time included the following:

- What was the future of public property going to be in the postsocialist era?
- Which means of acquiring extensive private property were legitimate? What was the extent of its inviolability?
- In which areas of life were market relations and private ownership, including ownership by foreign governments and individuals, going to be acceptable?

On these foundational matters, the country was polarized—not at all on the fringes but, rather, among the members of the most influential groups of Russian society, who had great economic, administrative, and media resources at their disposal. This polarization also affected the understanding of national sovereignty and its potential limits in relation to both the outside world and Russia's own citizens. Among other things, this included the fundamental concept of the boundaries between civil rights and national interests, as well as the limits of acceptable restrictions that could be imposed by government upon individual freedoms. In other words, society was polarized over issues that typically are not subject to political debates in competition-based systems because they reflect a consensus among the elites that has emerged over the course of history and that cannot and should not depend upon the outcomes of a popular vote.

This is the issue of the "limits of democracy"—the determination of what can and what cannot be subject to debate or used as a tool of adversarial competition among rival groups within a competition-based system. In principle, the existence and normal functioning of a competition-based political system requires and depends upon this issue having been resolved, and it requires having mechanisms in place that ensure adherence to a consensus about it. If there is no such consensus within the ruling class or among the sum total of a country's elites, then a competition-based political system becomes impossible—at least beyond the time frame of a single electoral cycle.

An unbiased and dispassionate analysis of all available experience in this area indicates that competition-based political systems function in a sustainable and relatively efficient manner if the issues put on the agenda and raised in election campaigns by competing political groups do not affect the foundations of a given society and do not destabilize its core. The opposite is also true: the wider and the deeper the disagreements among the various parts of the politically influential part of society (the stratum that, in the West, is usually called the "political class"), the greater the motivation of the currently ruling group to deny its competitors the opportunity to overturn the choice that was made by the voters in the previous election cycle. And if these disagreements affect the most essential, most fundamental, and most vital relations in society, then the willingness of the elites to accept free and universal voting as the supreme authority in political disputes may become infinitesimally low.[6]

This one reason is already enough to explain why it was highly unlikely that Russia in the early 1990s would develop a classical competition-based political system with all its democratic attributes, such as law-abiding political parties, relatively neat forms of political rivalry, and a fair tallying of election results with unpredictable outcomes. The gulf separating various groups within Russia's political class from each other, in terms of their views on how Russian society should be organized in the future and what its intermediate and long-range interests should be, was just too wide for this to happen. Incidentally, this is precisely why the competition-based system took hold and got off the ground in the Baltic states formerly under Soviet rule—in spite of all the difficulties and failures and even though, truthfully, the capitalism that they gained back is of a peripheral type—while in Russia and in most other former Soviet countries it did not happen.

This was arguably the central factor in the logic of the formation of an authoritarian instead of a competition-based political system in the 1990s in Russia. But it was undoubtedly reinforced by other factors as well. In particular, even since the beginning of the twentieth century, the development of government institutions in Russia increasingly lagged behind the developmental needs of society and behind the understanding on the part the educated portion of society that articulated those needs. Despite the fact that Russian society was prepared for a leap toward modernization and had realistic chances to accomplish it, at a certain point, the institutions of governance froze, proving to be too rigid, and thus did not let those chances materialize. By the start of the twentieth century, the outdated character of those institutions was acting as a brake upon the country's economic and political development. To an extent, this backwardness of political forms was the root and cause of the acute crisis of 1917–1918, which turned out to be too much for Russian statehood at the time to handle. The outcome of it was a tragic period, when Russia was subjected to a brutal and unsuccessful experiment in constructing a nonmarket economy with a totalitarian political superstructure.

In the late 1980s, that experiment came to an end, yet the backwardness of Russia's political forms, which had been the major contributing factor behind that experiment, was still there. Moreover, the political system of post-Soviet Russia reproduced not just the many flaws of the Soviet system but also those of the pre-Soviet, pre-Bolshevik institutions of imperial Russia. These flaws included excessive centralization of power, inadequate feedback loops, a lack of balance among various institutions, insensitivity of the authorities to the changing needs and demands of society, and the lack of effective mechanisms of parliamentary control over the executive (in post-1993 Russia, the president's powers, whether informal or officially established, have been nearly monarchical, unrestrained by either law or political practice). Furthermore, the powers that be are not in the habit of looking for reasonable compromises that would open up space for social and political transformations without antagonizing significant strata and forces in society. There also is no habit of replacing individuals in power on a regular basis and on the grounds of an unbiased assessment of the outcomes of their work.

All these congenital flaws in Russia's political development, dating back as far as the beginning of the twentieth century, were reenacted in the course of its post-Soviet reconstruction. This was exacerbated by the drastic decline in the educational and cultural standards of Russia's political class, compared to pre-Soviet times. The seventy-year-long Soviet era largely undermined what could have become the economic foundations of a competition-based political system: the presence of various groups of large property owners who would be willing and able to support rival political teams capable of acting as the key protagonists in legal political competition.

Moreover, for a long period of time, Russians had no idea about any forms of property ownership other than personal or state ownership. Thus, the emergence of a stratum of individuals who might view themselves as full-fledged, legitimate owners of private property, having not only the right but also the responsibility to take active part in civic and political life in terms of having a seat at the table rather than being "on the menu," would require time, robust public debate, and even educational efforts.

At the outset of the Soviet era, the propertied classes of private owners, such as landed gentry, merchants, industrialists, and even affluent peasants (who had just barely gained the feeling of being the actual owners of the land that they tilled) were destroyed, not just as "economic classes" but also literally, by physical extermination. From the standpoint of what I have said about the need for a propertied class to sustain political competition, this disaster had immense negative implications, including implications for the political consciousness of the country's population. There were no economic groups that could become an adequate substitute to those classes in every sense of it—not small semiprivate cooperative traders of the late

Soviet period; not the so-called red directors, the government-appointed managers of large production units on the eve of privatization (who all of a sudden gained power over vast industrial and agricultural assets while having only tangential relationship to the prior development of these public assets); not the beneficiaries of the "small-business privatization" of the early 1990s, that is, former managers of small Soviet-era trading firms, construction business, and services; and certainly not the former criminal and semicriminal elements (including petty black market peddlers and managers of large clandestine networks) that rose up from the de facto underground and attempted to seize control of the most lucrative opportunities in commercial distribution and finance.

The last Soviet generation grew up and came of age at a time when the totalitarian state, personified by whichever individual was in charge at the top, was in total control of the country's assets in their entirety, both by law and in practice. There was no way they could accept these newly emerging groups of propertied people as legitimate owners, empowered to handle the enormous assets at their discretion, let alone trust them to use those assets as an instrument for defending their political interests. Even wealthy people themselves could not feel at ease in this capacity—both because of their worldview, which was shaped by the total monopolism of the Soviet system, and because of the hostility they felt from the bulk of the population. The majority of Russians persisted in their belief that there were no "sacred rights of property" in the country prior to and independent of the country's highest ruler and his benevolent attitude.

This view of the country's top authority as the only legitimate source of property rights, especially for large-scale industrial and agricultural assets, survived even the tumultuous period of the early 1990s and has persisted into the subsequent stages of the post-Soviet era. In those stages, as Russia's central government rediscovered its strength, it began to actively reinforce those stereotypes in society by transmitting, directly or indirectly, the message that all other sources of property ownership were a form of banditry and a theft of property from the people.

This, in turn, has made it psychologically impossible for most Russians to separate the functions and powers of government authority from the functions and powers of that sole individual who is ensconced at the top of the pyramid of power. This also leads to ascribing to this individual powers and capabilities that he does not possess in reality. Another consequence is that the authorities and their supporters effectively deny any opposition groups or individual politicians the right to use government resources in their struggle for power against the dominant group. Neither this ruling circle nor Russian society at large find the authorities' monopolistic control of the distribution of all key resources in the country to be unnatural or unacceptable, let alone criminal. To the contrary, they sanctify this monopolistic power by the use of tradition, drawing upon a variety of "religious" and "historical" justifications. The implicit underlying message is that this single-handed control over all resources is the natural form of organization and functioning of the powers that be. This alone is sufficient to present a daunting challenge to anyone who would try to establish a workable system of governmental checks and balances built upon the suitable economic foundation of autonomous groups of large and small property owners.

It is also here that we can find the roots of the understanding of strong power as being completely unrestrained by anything or anybody. People have been viewing efforts to establish a genuine separation of powers as attempts to weaken government authority, to disable it, to impose an alien will upon it. In this regard, the demeaning powerlessness of Russia's present-day parliament is largely a product of the campaign of vilification of legislative authority that was waged, spontaneously or not, by Russia's leading mass media in the 1990s. Let us not forget that, back then, the journalists who viewed themselves as supporters of Russia's "democratic choice" frantically portrayed Russia's representative institutions, first the Supreme Soviet and then the State Duma, as useless and as burdensome chains shackling our "mighty" first president, Boris Yeltsin, and allegedly impeding his attempts to charge ahead with the socioeconomic reforms that they said the country needed. Even the courts (to the extent that they retained some degree of political significance) were now and then portrayed in the media as pesky obstacles on Russia's road to "economic reforms."

Unfortunately, in Russia's history, the understanding of the supreme power as the function of an equilibrium among diverse societal forces, and of a compromise among them, was minimal. Most of Russia's public opinion typically viewed any compromise as "rotten," as something that could and should be discarded as soon as possible and without any compunction. Russian society today is arguably paying a high price for stereotypes and preconceptions that, by and large, were shaped by Russia's history.

Finally, another factor that influenced the political situation in Russia in the 1990s was the international environment.[7] I believe that, in spite of all of the inertia and other idiosyncrasies of the mind-set of the Russian public, there was a relatively brief period in the late 1980s and early 1990s when popular disillusionment with the Soviet societal order and way of life was so deep and so widespread that there was an opportunity to drastically transform that mind-set. Russians' views of different sets of power relationships than the ones that had been historically present and embedded in the Russian consciousness would have been different today, had the former Cold War enemies of the Soviet Union been ready to respond to the country's abandonment of its ideological dogmas, and of the Cold War, by looking for ways to include the Soviet Union in the existing world order on terms that would be seen by Russia's political class and most of its citizens as dignified. Of course, in and of itself, this would have provided no guarantees of the development of Russia's political system along a nonauthoritarian path. Yet it would have been a weighty consideration in Russia's process of selecting its subsequent path of development.

In reality, however, the prevailing response in the West to the tectonic political shifts that occurred in the Soviet Union was shortsighted and selfish. The political shift was viewed as merely an opportunity to get rid of an old irritant, the widely acknowledged need to pursue a complex and multifaceted policy of "containing" the Soviets. Western leaders immediately paid the highest symbolic honors to the leaders of Russia by recognizing Russia as a diplomatic successor to the USSR at every level. Yet, at the same time, having lost a practical interest in developing a rational framework of relationships, as it had done with the Soviet Union, the West began to marginalize Russia in various contexts, both as a country and as a people.

In its relationships with the West, Russia's political class encountered nakedly egotistic disregard for lofty principles, in practice, which was unfortunately justified as "realpolitik." This was an important factor (though not the only one) in strengthening Russian skepticism about the liberal, competition-based model of political order. It convinced Russia's political class that feigning competitive politics and liberal institutions (such as the separation of powers, free elections, and the replacement of individuals in power on a regular basis) was just as "marketable" to its Western partners as the hard, conscientious work to actually establish them. The reason for the failure of the West to become a factor of genuine modernization in the Russian political and economic system after the collapse of the Soviet Union is a debatable issue. However, in my view, it relates both to the short-sightedness or incompetence of individual political leaders and to the overall crisis of political mentality and behavior in recent decades.[8]

Whatever the case, in the 1990s, a wide array of factors shaped the political system of the "new" post-Soviet Russia in such a way as to make it authoritarian, averse to innovation, limited in its efficacy, and devoid of incentives to move in the direction of an alternative liberal, competition-based order.

In concluding our review of the 1990s, let us briefly sum up the determinants and the factors that led to the formation of the present-day authoritarianism of a peripheral type, as they emerged from the reforms of those years. With some caveats in mind, we can identify three groups of factors. The first among them was the sequence of events that led to the emergence of a system based upon the fusion of governmental power with the ownership of economic assets. This sequence included the hyperinflation (the government's expropriation of savings) of 1992, the crime-ridden privatization (the loans-for-shares auctions) of 1995–1997, and election fraud and the subjugation of the media in 1996–1998.

The second factor was the Bolshevik methods used by the reformers. Reforms and decision-making were done on the basis of such tenets as "The ends justify the means," "The economic basis [the character of property relations] will nearly automatically determine the superstructure [the shape of legal and civic institutions]," "The primitive accumulation of capital is always crime-ridden," and so on.

The third group of factors was related to the authorities' refusal to reassess Soviet-era history, to pass judgment at the governmental level on the legacy of Stalinism and Bolshevism. This refusal gave rise to Russia's crisis of self-identification, as people found themselves disoriented with regard to basic values; it resulted in a mishmash of ideologies, in the flourishing of defiant ignorance presented as the so-called Eurasianist ideology; and ultimately it made it impossible for Russia to define its place in the world in a historically grounded and logical manner. As a result, by the late 1990s, Russians were in the throes of pervasive disillusionment, confusion, and a sense of having been utterly deceived. They were increasingly searching for answers to their problems by looking to the past, to the Soviet era. This was the context in which Vladimir Putin entered the stage.

However, as I have noted, the 1990s was a time when the present system was barely emerging and was still taking shape. Some of its traits were still a work in progress, while others were not yet even perceptible. Therefore, the first decade of the twenty-first century was no less important to the formation of the present-day version of Russia's authoritarianism. We shall now address the developments of this period in more detail.

2000–2010: WHAT HAPPENED TO THE POLITICAL SYSTEM

I shall begin my analysis of what happened to Russia's political system in the first decade of this century by reiterating the central point of the previous section: in the 1990s, Russia was not developing along a democratic path. In this context, democracy is understood as a type of political organization that includes:

1. a distribution of power resources among several centers and groups within the system;

2. an effective separation of powers into different branches that function to preclude a concentration of power in the hands of a single person; and
3. the use of elections as a means to resolve political disputes and tensions and to select the next governing team from among several contenders.

In the 1990s, Russia did not progress in any noticeable way along any of these three dimensions; every attempt to prove the opposite has been unconvincing. During that particular period, in my opinion, the formal indicators of political democracy in the aforementioned sense of this term were in their sorriest state. They were virtually entirely emptied of their substantive content, and the institutions of democracy were being discredited, while the thick layer of demagogic rhetoric generated spontaneous protest among broad swaths of Russian society.

In addition, by the late 1990s the mechanisms of governance as such, and especially its administrative hierarchy, were in a truly sorry state as well. There was a broad consensus that the authorities of the Russian state were failing to perform the basic functions of governance that are essential under any type of a political system, such as maintaining public order, keeping track of its assets and protecting its citizens, preserving the integrity of the legal regulation of social and economic relations across Russia's territory, making the court system work properly, producing and executing the country's budget, and so on. Instead, government was being supplanted in these key functions by spontaneous, elemental forces, with plain violence used as a tool of competition, semicriminal unwritten arrangements taking the place of laws, and the like.

Therefore, after the transfer of power from Yeltsin to Putin, when the Kremlin suddenly launched a virtual campaign of denunciation of the "unruly 1990s," it looked from the outside as if it was actually going to target the very failures of that decade that I have outlined. Although this quasi campaign was to a large extent demagogic, it also undoubtedly built upon a genuine sense that the Russian state had been unacceptably weakened in both external and, most importantly, domestic matters. It cannot be denied that, by the year 2000, Russian society and its bureaucratic elite were in a sense demanding a consolidation of governance. This was supposed to bring more order into everyday life by strengthening the state—not by making the state bigger or more ferocious in its use of force but rather by making it effective in performing those functions that make a society modern, sophisticated, and open to development.

How the system responded to this demand is a different story. Instead of consolidating the essential formative functions of the state, the system consolidated the authoritarian power at the top. As a result, Russia's authoritarianism morphed into its present-day shape, projecting demodernization, conservative chauvinism, and isolationism.

To put it differently, if, during the early and mid-1990s, Russia's post-Soviet political system passed the first of its developmental crossroads by opting for an authoritarian model of development over a competition-based one, during the next decade it passed a second major road fork as well. This time, it was a choice between a modernizing type of authoritarianism, a kind of "authoritarianism for the sake of progress," and a conservative, stagnation-prone type of authoritarianism. The conservative type begins by erecting barriers on the path of any change that might weaken the ruling circle's control over society—though eventually, at the final stage of its existence, this control is lost because of the degeneration of the institutions that enable governance in the first place.[9]

Strictly speaking, this is about a paradox that is well-known from history. It is expressed by the ages-old dictum "Everything must change so that everything stays the same." The sustainability of any political system, including an authoritarian one, ultimately depends upon its dynamism and its ability to adapt, to open space for the growth of new forces and relationships, to detect shifts in a situation and to come up with responses to the new threats and challenges resulting from these changes. In theory, a competition-based system has significant advantages in this regard, because it assumes (again in theory) that the political team that fails to recognize an objective need for change will inevitably be defeated in the elections.

Of course, in reality nothing is so unequivocal. The need for changes is not always self-evident, the mechanisms do not operate automatically, and election outcomes may be very different from the system's objective needs in terms of survival and development. For its part, under certain conditions, an authoritarian system also may display flexibility, ability to adapt to changing circumstances, and commitment to genuine rather than phony achievements. Thus, an authoritarian government does not invariably have to result in its own fossilization, becoming a shackle on society and an obstacle to progress. Such outcomes are more likely to be a product of a combination of situational variables and the political inadequacy of the ruling circle.

It is difficult to determine the extent to which these two factors shape the outcome of the process. But this typically results in a regime that is on the defensive against multiple real and fictitious enemies, including those from abroad. Such a regime tries to impede the activities of any forces that it views as unfamiliar and puzzling. By doing this, it precludes the possibility of an evolutionary development of those institutions that are currently in place.

What happens next is more or less clear: the institutions that are incapable of changing, including changes to close the gap between themselves and the changing sociopolitical environment, will sooner or later be unable to perform the functions that have been assigned to them. Thus, police are no longer fighting crime in earnest, intelligence agencies are no longer combating threats to national sovereignty with the same resolve as before, tax collectors are no longer as determined to pursue actual tax evaders. The courts in such a system acquire some traits of "independence"—not from the control of the supreme authorities but rather from any public control whatsoever—and by and large become commercialized. Legislative bodies pass their bills chaotically, without giving any thought to the laws' implications or to the difficulties involved in making them work in practice. The agencies responsible for investing public funds under this system may follow any kind of logic whatsoever, except for the logic of stimulating economic growth, and most often they do whatever is convenient and serve someone's private interest in spending public funds.

As a result of all this, the government at its highest level essentially loses the most effective tools for influence upon the situation in the country, and then its future gets determined by the forces of inertia and by various contingencies, including (and perhaps primarily) contingencies of external origin. Therefore, at a certain stage, an authoritarian government with a conservatively chauvinistic ideology and without the goal of modernization and reform is bound to become hostage to its changing environment, and this environment may either keep the government afloat for quite an extensive period or make an acute political crisis inevitable, with the regime in question being incapable of overcoming or surviving such a crisis.

During the first decade of our century, Russia passed the turning point that was mentioned earlier, the moment of choice between putting effort into modernization or building new fences and barriers on the path of political changes that might potentially threaten the stability of the authorities—and thus blocking any meaningful political development whatsoever. Today, the implications of having passed that turning point are evident to almost everyone. But, fifteen years ago, in the course of the presidential campaign of 2000, I was hardly able to persuade anyone that this kind of future was on the horizon, in spite of the very high likelihood of this course of events, given the characteristics of the oligarchical system that had been established in Russia, the personality of Boris Yeltsin's successor, Vladimir Putin, and the means by which he was brought to power.

Certainly, all the determinants of the outcome that is with us today were also present at the time. First of all, there was the absence of a powerful class of legitimate owners of large-scale productive economic assets like those that qualify as "big business" in any Western country, a class that would be willing and able to play a significant role in defining the political future of the country. As some will object by mentioning the "oligarchs" of the 1990s and their active politicking at the time, let me say the following.

The oligarchs were not an economic class. It is true that a few dozen Russians became real owners of exorbitant personal wealth, and that they also became formal owners of one or two hundred of the most desirable economic assets of 1990s Russia, such as oil companies Yukos, Sibneft, Lukoil, and Surgutneftegas; steel mills like Mechel or NLMK; nickel and copper giant Norilsk Nickel; and so on. Yet they were unable to coalesce into an enduring class of people who would be aware of their shared interests—essentially national interests—and who would be bound together by both shared and personal interests in the development of Russia's economy and society along the path of what is often called market democracy. They could not become such a class because they ended up in their "oligarchic" roles by accident, because they had neither a shared history nor a significant track record in business, and, finally, because there were so few of them. Members of the group were not allies sharing the same interests but rather strangers laying claims to a portion of a limited number of desirable assets— assets that the new authorities had ended up with and were now doling out to others as they saw fit.

Second, they were not viewed as legitimate property holders by the political establishment, by the population, or even by themselves. I may have written about it a thousand times, but I am prepared to reiterate the point once more: A property right is not a sealed piece of paper and is not a record made in some registry by the officials in charge. A property right is, first and foremost, the willingness of the society and its institutions to acknowledge the right of a given person to make decisions about a particular economic asset at one's discretion, including decisions about selling it, passing it on as inheritance, or doing with it anything else that is not restricted or prohibited by law. But the oligarchs did not have this kind of broad recognition of their property rights (nor, fifteen years later, do the present-day holders of large economic assets have this).[10]

This is precisely why the oligarchs as a group could not become the driving force for modernizing reforms—or even provide reliable support for such reforms, should the government decide to initiate them. The example of Mikhail Khodorkovsky, the businessman who supposedly advocated large-scale political and social reforms, is completely irrelevant here. His political ambitions at the beginning of the century were of a personal nature rather than reflecting the collective aspirations of an economic class. His pro-modernization rhetoric became so central to his pronouncements largely as a result of his showdown with the authorities; the cause-and-effect relationship between this rhetoric and his relations with the Kremlin is by no means as simple as some tend to believe.[11] Small and medium-size business owners had even less of a chance to become a political fulcrum of an authoritarian modernization during the late 1990s, given how socially and ideologically disparate and politically disorganized they were.

On the other hand, the central government bureaucracy was somewhat better prepared to assume that role. And, paradoxical as it may seem, it did for a quite a while sustain the possibility of a turn of the authoritarian system toward more recognition of society's interests and needs. However, in the end, the "modernizer" faction turned out to be too politically weak to influence the policies of the Kremlin in a fundamental way. As a result, these policies ended up being nearly the opposite of those advocated by the modernizers in the bureaucracy, and representatives of this stripe who opted to stay aboard ended up being hostages of the course of action that was chosen by Vladimir Putin.

At about this same time, prices for oil and gas rose to unprecedented heights in the international markets, in both absolute and relative terms. I believe that, surprising as it may seem, this was yet another important reason why an authoritarian modernization did not take place in Russia. Some may view this explanation as too simplistic, and yet, at times, complex social phenomena may be based on really simple things. It is not at all surprising that the rapid growth of the financial reserves of both the government and of Russia's population largely deprived them of the incentive to pursue modernizing policies that would be complex and risky (in terms of how different strata in Russian society might have responded to them). Instead, the accumulation of wealth favored a different priority: not to do anything that might disturb this transitory stability.

Meanwhile, the rise in prices for Russia's export commodities was stopped by the global financial crisis of 2008–2009. Russia's authorities responded by instinctively retreating into a cocoon and setting up barriers to separate themselves from the ups and downs of Western economies and their complex mechanisms of growth. This was achieved through the rejection of "unnecessary" socioeconomic experimentation and by relying upon the tried-and-tested routines of the resource-based economy—namely, pumping hydrocarbons from newly found deposits and building mega pipelines for their delivery. This became the primary content of economic policies at home.

By now, even a serious prospect of unfavorable trends for Russia's commodities on the world energy market cannot compel its political system to embark on a pursuit of ways to modernize the economy. Even though the situation was rather different during the first years of the new century, the protracted period of windfall revenues gained without much hard work most likely was a major factor that helped conservative, anti-reform policies to prevail, apparently for the long haul.

Likewise, the personal characteristics of the members of Russia's ruling circle may have played a considerable role in tipping the scale in this particular direction. These personal characteristics include wariness about the outside world and a misunderstanding of the ways in which Western politics operate and how this shapes the West's stance vis-à-vis the rest of the world, including Russia. These traits among the Russian leadership caused it to vastly overstate the risks of the wider opening of

Russia to the outside world through modernizing reforms. The Russian ruling elite's exaggeration of the importance of Russia to Western politicians led them to overstate the West's willingness and readiness to expend huge amounts of resources to bring Russia to a "single common denominator" on every political issue. Of course, this exaggeration of the threat of outside interference in Russia's politics was caused in part by domestic considerations, but it would be wrong to view it as merely a tool of manipulating public opinion. The authorities were quite genuinely alarmed by the specter of a powerful political force willing to stage a "regime change" operation in exchange for relatively modest financial reward, even if that fear was out of proportion with the actual extent of the threat.[12]

At the same time, one has to admit that Western leaders did not make any effort to assuage the Russian government's fears and concerns. No one made it a point to really convince Russian authorities that the various grants for the "development of democracy," which were being issued to opposition-minded individuals and organizations perceived as democrats by the American and European public, were not part of a full-scale plot to topple the Russian government. Even if Russian authorities firmly believed in Western conspiracies, they possibly could have been convinced by the (perhaps somewhat cynical) argument that various nongovernmental organization grants to Russian pro-Western opposition groups were just about as meager, formalistic, and unproductive as, for example, the aid that the Soviet Union, in its time, provided to Western communist parties. Anyone who thought that Soviet handouts to local communists and "leftists" would lead to a power shift in the United States would have been extremely naive; similarly, the whisperings about the billions of dollars that allegedly have been pumped into Russia through some (at times irrelevant and even fringe) nonprofit organizations, to be used to oust the ruling elite or to break up Russia, are just plain nonsense.

Of course, this is not to say that we must completely rule out any attempts by specific individuals and organizations outside Russia to influence the political situation within it in pursuit of their own commercial and other interests. But the risks associated with this cannot by any means be used to justify the rejection of reforms and an all-out confrontation with the outside world. Regrettably, at the beginning of the twenty-first century, there was no one willing or able to explain these truths to Russian authorities. To the contrary, some Western politicians thought it was quite innocuous to tease the Kremlin by making thunderous but empty speeches, semi-ritualistically invoking "support for democracy" in the post-Soviet space (but apparently not in such places as Turkmenistan or Tajikistan), as well as loudly talking about things like the upcoming new expansion of NATO to include former Soviet countries.

One way or another, between approximately 2000 and 2005, Russia's ruling circle opted for a conservative, anti-reform type of authoritarianism over a modernization-oriented variety. The authoritarianism that prevailed in Russia was not open to dialogue with independent domestic political currents of any significance or to collaboration with the Western world. And, with all the fine-print qualifications and short-term fluctuations in overall policies, this type of authoritarianism became firmly entrenched in Russia in the second half of the decade.

It was certainly a gradual and not an abrupt shift. Changes in the composition and the character of activities of such government institutions as the presidential staff, the State Duma, the Federation Council, local legislatures, and so forth accumulated for years before revealing their qualitative differences from the past. To the extent that an official state ideology transpired from relevant documents and speeches, it maintained the inertia of the 1990s, with reformist and modernization-oriented rhetoric, for quite some time. This rhetoric spiked for the last time during the period when Dmitry Medvedev occupied the presidential office (2008–2012).

Likewise, there were some ups and downs in the government's willingness to engage in dialogue with Russian civil society organizations from a broad ideological spectrum, as opposed to meeting with preselected and thoroughly vetted representatives. At times, it seemed as if the authorities were in the process of adjusting their prior policies or, at the very least, displaying some hesitation about the expediency of keeping those policies in place. Nevertheless, looking through the prism of medium-term trends, the choice made in the Kremlin was becoming more and more evident with every passing year.

The years that have passed since the so-called castling (popular Russian lingo for the set of decisions that moved Putin back into the presidency and Medvedev into the prime minister's office in the spring of 2012) have not merely reaffirmed the steadiness of the policies pursued by the ruling circle. This period also introduced significant new elements into this picture, and they deserve a separate analysis. But before giving more attention to these details, I shall outline a comprehensive picture of the political system that took shape in Russia, as a result of the aforementioned developments, over the course of the two post-Soviet decades.

3

AUTHORITARIANISM ON THE PERIPHERY

Understanding Russia's Political System and How It Works

The events of the twenty years following the collapse of the Soviet system have brought Russia to a political system that is based upon a monopolistic grip on power by one dominant group of the ruling bureaucracy. This group appoints whomever they want as chief executives of every uniformed agency (the military, police, security services, and so forth), every administrative unit, and every major economic institution.

This system precludes the replacement of the ruling circle without the simultaneous breakup of the entire system and a deep political crisis. This is a system geared toward its own self-perpetuation. It excludes the possibility of either spontaneously evolving or reforming itself in accordance with a changing environment. Finally, this is a system based upon the redistribution of rents derived from administrative power; therefore, it is interested in the preservation of those economic and societal conditions that enable it to extract and to keep these rents. I will discuss all the features and characteristics of this system in more detail in the rest of this chapter.

THE FORMULA OF DOMINATION

As I have noted, the primary feature that characterizes the formation and succession of the present-day power system in Russia is its authoritarianism. In its essence, if not in appearance, the current political system in Russia is an undiluted authoritarian regime. In this instance, I use this term without a negative emotional connotation. This is just an unbiased assessment of a system of power in which a narrow ruling circle (either with or without a single leader among them) has secured a monopolistic control over the pyramid of administrative power while preventing any significant concentration of political resources in the hands of any other group.

Under our present conditions, such control is secured through more or less effective management of those media that shape public opinion (or, more precisely, the component of public opinion that is relevant for the authorities) as well as meticulous surveillance of all large-scale capital flows inside and into the country. The objective is to prevent any political groups or opposition structures that might be potentially dangerous for the ruling circle from accumulating any significant resources under their control. The tools that ensure achievement of this objective were identified and tested back in the 1990s. But it was over the following decade that this objective was placed at the center of government policies. Over time, it became not just increasingly more prominent but also, to a large extent, a goal in and of itself.

The quasi-corporate ruling circle put the political content of media resources, primarily public television and mass-circulation tabloids, under its control as early as the second half of the 1990s, essentially using these outlets as propaganda tools. One should not be misled by the fact that, in legal terms, some of these media were privately owned at the time. Already, the presidential staff and the narrow circle of the most influential members of the ruling group were playing key roles in deciding upon the political content transmitted by these media.

In the first years after the turn of the century, the ruling group decided to formalize and solidify this control through government ownership of most media resources. It started with the de facto nationalization of Vladimir Gusinsky's media empire and with the government asserting its full management authority over ORT, Russia's flagship TV channel. Following that, the government used proxy firms to secure ownership of virtually all mass media capable of shaping public perceptions of the substance and content of Russia's political life.

So far, over the period of Putin's rule since the turn of the century, this policy has allowed for the existence of individual opposition-minded media outlets, primarily online. However, these are viewed by the ruling circle as reflecting the feelings and opinions of a negligible fringe that is unable to impact the country's situation in any fundamental way. Thus, the opportunity to express pro-opposition sentiments and views has been restricted to those niche media channels that the authorities see as having only marginal influence. These media do not undermine or weaken the authorities' ability to control the minds of the larger strata of society, which could have been used by competing political groups as a weapon in their struggle.

The other pathway to ensuring the Kremlin's hold over political resources in the country has been the strengthening of its ability to control the flows of money that might be used for political aims, mainly for the formation of alternative centers of gravity in Russian politics. The prosecution in 2003 of Mikhail Khodorkovsky, one of the biggest beneficiaries of the Yeltsin-era "shares for loans" privatization, was the first show of the government's resolve not to allow any large-scale financial—and therefore organizational—resources outside of its purview to get involved in political struggle. It showed that all financial flows of any significance were going to be as tightly supervised as possible. There obviously were additional motivations involved in arresting and prosecuting Khodorkovsky, such as the fear of letting certain economic assets of strategic importance to slip away from government control, the personal economic interests of individual members of the ruling circle, and the poor personal relationship between Khodorkovsky and Putin. Yet the principal rationale was to show that, from now on, big money was not going to provide access to high-level politics, and, moreover, it was not going to serve its owners as a guarantee of immunity from prosecution and arrest.

From then on, the authorities became more and more determined to curb rich Russians' opportunities to use their personal fortunes toward political activities outside of government control. In practice, this was pursued primarily through the "ruling party," United Russia. The party assumed the functions of a vertical supervisory authority, extending from Moscow into the country's periphery. It has been charged with tracking the political activities of regional business owners and integrating them into the unified system of the authoritarian state while resolutely blocking any attempts to organize or to fund social and political projects that have not gained the consent of vertical hierarchy of power. The changes the Kremlin has made in the electoral system—namely, the abolition of gubernatorial elections in the regions and the election of regional legislatures by party slates only—were also intended to help achieve the task of full control over all political resources. At least in theory, this made it more difficult to use funds outside of government control to increase one's political influence.

Naturally, as in any such matter, the goal was never completely achieved; after all, the interests and tenets of the centralized vertical hierarchy seen in Russian politics often yield to the private interests, ambitions, and personal preferences of regional hacks and bureaucrats. Yet, overall, the authorities were quite consistent in stifling all unsanctioned political activities through administrative decisions about the use of financial resources (and at times through criminal prosecution). By now, these policies have become one of the linchpins of the power system in the country.

All the government rhetoric about the need to privatize large government holdings in the banking and resource industries, however practical this rhetoric might have seemed at times, have remained empty talk. This shows the steadiness of the authorities' policy of control over all those resources that could be put to political use by others. Moreover, during the first decade of the century, the state's directly or indirectly controlled share of cash flows tied to the banking sector and resource industries (virtually the only two truly significant streams of money in the Russian economy) has ostensibly grown in size.

The reason for the continuous postponement of the privatization of these two sectors is exclusively political, as there is no practical economic or even ideological rationale for delaying it. Preventing politically ambitious groups other than themselves from using the resources of banks or big resource companies to fuel their own growth has been the primary concern of the upper crust of government bureaucracy. And maintaining a direct government grip on the largest corporations in these two sectors reduces the likelihood that some part of the cash flows they control might be used for political activities that have not been approved by the federal government, or for activities that directly confront the government's interests and goals.

Herein, too, lies the most likely explanation for the failures to launch political campaigns using private financial fortunes, even when the initiators of those projects were extremely cautious and deferential to the system. Even though, as a rule, such endeavors were initiated by and undertaken with the consent of members of the ruling circle, sooner or later (and usually fairly soon) these budding politicians tended to fall prey to palace intrigues and ended up being shut down by external pressure before gaining any traction. And the real reason for this is not the lack of funds or organizational talent but rather that the logic of an authoritarian power does not leave any room, in principle, for even concealed, undercover competition for the place that is held by the ruling group.

Having placed domestic sources of political funding under its control, the Kremlin became more active in its efforts to block attempts to use foreign funds for this purpose. These foreign sources had in fact been placed under government watch and partial control previously, but it was finally done openly and in public in 2012. New laws created the official status of "foreign agent" as well as special reporting and accountability procedures for nongovernmental nonprofit organizations that were funded from abroad and whose activities had a political dimension. At the same time, a government-issued regulation blocked any research institutions and teams from obtaining foreign grants without government sanction.

Finally, this array of measures was complemented by the law that prohibited legislators and high-ranking officials (that is, all those members of Russia's elite who were potentially capable of initiating political or related activities without government consent, or of becoming deeply involved in such activities) from having bank accounts or other financial assets outside of the country. Even though, formally speaking, the law is intended to shield influential government officials from potential vulnerability to foreign influence, in reality this so-called nationalization of the elites is an effective means of control over the possibility that some government officials might fund political activities out of the government's view—regardless of any foreign interests whatsoever. The fact that the passing of this law coincided with other actions intended to block autonomous sources of funding for political activities suggests that the Kremlin's primary concern in passing this law was not the risk of manipulations on the part of foreign intelligence agencies but rather the threat presented by autonomous political activities within the elite but outside of the control of the ruling circle.

As a result of these government-initiated moves, any individuals or groups with political ambitions who aren't sanctioned and controlled by the authorities cannot count on any significant financial support, at least within the current legal framework. This certainly makes it much easier for the ruling circle to achieve its goal of maintaining its monopolistic grip on power. It also makes it unnecessary to resort to outright criminal prosecution of oppositionists—except for those inclined to take part in boisterous street actions with sometimes unpredictable consequences.

Naturally, in real life things get more complicated. Government control is not always absolute, while human imperfections drive the system or its individual representatives toward excessive cruelty, toward carrying the persecution of its opponents beyond what would be rational from its own point of view. Yet, overall, the ruling circle's control over key assets and cash flows in the economy is quite effective in performing its function of maintaining the "political stability" as they envision it.

As mentioned, the other instrument used to ensure the ruling circle's monopolistic grip on power is its tight hold upon the tools of influence over the mass consciousness. At present, the most important among these tools are nationwide TV channels and regional mass media. Taken together, these outlets, to a great extent, shape the perceptions of a very large number of Russian adults about the world around them, and they play a decisive role in programming citizens' social and political behavior.

This certainly does not mean that people accept as an article of faith everything that is foisted upon them by these media. Much of it, and first and foremost the propagated image of the government as the defender of the people's interests, is viewed by a great many people with much skepticism and even scorn. Mass opinion of officialdom and of the moral character of the ruling bureaucracy, including its top brass, is widely known. It is not an appreciative view, to put it mildly, whatever the official media might say. However, the single most important goal of the authorities turns out to be fully achievable—imposing their information agenda upon the country and thus identifying linchpins in the mass consciousness upon which the relative political security of the ruling circle can be anchored.[1]

Nonetheless, the ruling circle do not necessarily need to have total, comprehensive, and all-encompassing control over these media outlets. Unlike totalitarian systems, which seek to assert complete dominance over the minds of the people, authoritarian systems do not set such grandiose goals for themselves. In their set of priorities, the principal task of their policies with regard to the channels of mass communication is to preclude the possibility that other groups—their potential rivals in the struggle for power and influence—might use these channels in the pursuit of their own goals, which may be incompatible with those of the ruling circle.

Preventing this does not require that the rulers try to reeducate society in line with some coherent value-based ideology. It is enough to infuse society with the sense that there is no alternative to the status quo and that this status quo is not, so to speak, jeopardizing their future. In other words, it is enough to persuade the bulk of the population that the present order is natural and acceptable, while the opposition's promises of something better, more just, or more efficient is empty talk that comes from an evil source.

To ascertain this, one may just look at the content of the government-controlled media production and compare it with, for example, that of Soviet times. In contrast to Soviet-era media, today's main government-controlled TV channels do not attempt to lecture the people about what to believe and how to behave. The national TV shows with the largest audience share today would not have passed the filter of Soviet-era censorship, not only on political and ideological but also on ethical and aesthetic grounds. Even the so-called political broadcasting mostly contains almost no positive messaging at all. Its only function is to discredit any alternative whatsoever to the powers that be. This is achieved by portraying other contenders for power as at least as selfish as its present holders but also socially (or ethnically) alien to most of the population.

One way or another, all the media governed by the ruling circle feed their consumers with two principal messages. The first is that nothing that is happening in the country is extraordinary or destabilizing; the status quo is here to stay, and everything that is going on is under control and will not end up in anything catastrophic. The second message is that there is no alternative whatsoever to the current state of affairs and that anybody who says the opposite is either a liar, a foreign mercenary—in either case, a disgusting and completely selfish creature—or, in rare cases, an absolutely naive daydreamer who has lost all touch with reality.

At the same time, outside of the framework of the political duties assigned to the relevant media, there is unrestricted space for a full diversity of opinion—all the way to its most preposterous forms and expressions, which undermine the very basics of human coexistence in society. And, of course, the existence of the media's political requirement does not preclude the freedom of commercial activities, which in most instances is accepted as a given, implying that the managers of Kremlin-controlled mass media are expected to use their power for personal enrichment and prosperity. Moreover, the rapid enrichment of these media managers at the expense of the government as the owner of these major media channels is, for all intents and purposes, welcomed by the ruling circle, and at times even initiated by it, as a reward for the managers' loyalty and readiness to serve the rulers without any compunction.

Granted, the stream of media messaging set in motion by these manipulative tools does not produce a large mass of authentic supporters of the ruling circle. Yet it performs another, much more important function. Namely, it inculcates the huge mass of Russians with the sense that there is no other kind of life beyond the media agenda that is being imposed on them, that any alternative whatsoever to the political realities of the present is just an inferior replica of the status quo, and that the lies and hypocrisy in the media's portrayal of reality is not a deviation but rather a universal fixture of civic and political activities as such.

Let me reiterate: this way of managing mass media cannot secure society's active support for the ruling circle. But, most importantly, it does ensure a societal attitude of scornful indifference toward any attempts to secure support for any group or team seeking to a become a political alternative to the ruling circle. And, in terms of safeguarding the existing system of rule in present-day Russia, general passivity, skepticism, and indifference toward politics guarantees stability better than explicit support by socially active groups of the population. This is so, in part, because enthusiastic public support must be constantly fueled by tangible successes and achievements, whereas maintaining an attitude of indifference and the sense that real changes in the country are impossible to achieve does not require excessive effort or expenditure.

Clearly, this way of governing the country yields satisfactory results only under relatively stable conditions, absent any external shocks or unmanageable domestic crises. These kinds of tools may be useful in averting small-scale trouble or tackling short-term challenges to authoritarian rule, but they are hardly helpful against major destructive, destabilizing forces. The tools make it more or less possible to cope with tactical problems in the short term, yet the state remains powerless in the face of strategic threats and powerful destructive trends, both internal and external. Society's dismissive attitude toward all political rhetoric neutralizes and emasculates every criticism of the authorities, making it impossible to remove specific individuals from power against their will. But these public attitudes also make it impossible for the authorities to survive truly critical conditions by mobilizing public support and obtaining cooperation from society. To the contrary, under such conditions, the masses will tacitly enjoy seeing the authorities' failure in a crisis situation, even if society as a whole suffers in the process. The instruments used to suppress societal threats to the authorities may work relatively well under a system that is sustained by the inertia of an orderly everyday life, yet they become powerless and unusable in the face of mass protracted challenges to the status quo. Nevertheless, at this time, the instruments used to sustain the Kremlin's monopolistic grip on power has been fully formed and is relatively effective in serving its purposes, from the point of view of the members of the ruling circle.

ELECTIONS WITHOUT A CHOICE

Within any authoritarian system of governance, by definition, elections are not intended to be used as an instrument to determine which group of people will gain access to the levers of governance. In such a system, the ruling circle as the highest authority is permanently in power as a matter of principle. Though the composition of this circle may—and is even bound to—change over time, internal personnel modifications are made by their always stable core membership and are never submitted for approval by anybody outside of that group.

Within institutions and agencies that compose the government bureaucracy, both in its narrow and in its broad sense, senior executive staff is filled through appointments by the higher-ups. The only possible exception to this rule is at the lowest layer of the government apparatus. Heads of local self-government in the municipalities are still elected by the people, but they have no significant resources or power. That is, essentially all personnel changes, even those that are not planned in advance and that occur by necessity, are handled internally by the vertical hierarchy of power, without seeking any consent whatsoever from other groups that may aspire to positions of governmental power. In this system of governance, elections are either not held at all or are merely a facade, used to give an official status to the personnel decisions that have already been made, as if stamping them with "public approval."

Naturally, in those instances when an authoritarian system uses the procedure of elections (whether because it has become an established tradition, to gain additional legitimacy, or for other reasons), the elections' main feature, and at the same time the precondition for their continued use, is the predictability of the outcome. This is achieved through controlling the electoral process, the tallying of the votes, and the official determination of their results. Controlling these processes means having the power to interfere with the process, but such interference is not the only effective way to achieve the needed results and, under certain conditions, may not be used in its crude and explicit forms, such as outright election fraud. Given that genuine competition with an unpredictable outcome already indicates that the system itself is competition-based, which is antithetical to authoritarian rule, the ruling circle responds to every decrease in the predictability of an outcome either by perfecting its methods of control or by abandoning the use of elections altogether.

This principle common to authoritarian systems also operates within those frameworks that formally allow for the existence of multiple political parties. In reality, such regimes allocate a certain number of slots within the system (mainly in its representative bodies) to parties that are not formally included in the vertical hierarchy of power. In exchange for agreeing to play by the system's rules, these parties obtain some rather meager share of political resources, such as occasional opportunities to influence some secondary aspects of government decisions, and some perks for the leadership of these parties, like those enjoyed by high-ranking officials (welfare packages, special pension arrangements, an indulgent attitude toward conflicts of interest, and the like). Also, as part of the establishment they can count on lifelong employment in a safe and privileged position.

Essentially, all these features have been replicated within the political system that has taken shape in recent decades in Russia. Although the means of filling vacancies in the power system, at every level and in every one of its facets, are typical of an authoritarian regime, Russia nonetheless continues to hold elections for the positions of the chief executive—at the national level, at the level of municipal and village administrations, and, if the recent trend continues, at the regional level. (Though the elections of regional governors were abolished in 2004, they were partially restored in 2012, even if in a truncated form.) Russia also continues to hold elections to the legislative assemblies at different levels of government. Even though the role of representative bodies in a mature authoritarian system is minuscule, their preservation is closely tied to the existence of political parties, for without elected representative institutions, the existence of parties becomes utterly pointless, not just in practice but also in a formal sense.

Over the past twenty years, political parties in modern Russia, along with the political system as a whole, have gone through a complex evolution—from associations established with the goal of acceding to power in the country, mainly through elections and associated procedures, to subordinate elements within the authoritarian power system. As such, they perform the functions that were assigned to them within the overall framework of such a system and in accordance with its rules.[2] I do not mean that the role played by these marginal parties (largely not by their own volition) is fixed once and for all. If the situation in Russia were to change for the worse, or even for the better, all those unspoken bargains would immediately become inoperative. Then the activities of these parties may very quickly acquire a fundamentally different character and their focus may shift to new priorities. At present, however, the party structure continues to operate within the framework imposed on it by the authoritarian system—as does the institution of elections to which the present and the future of political parties is inextricably bound.

It is hard to say to what extent the present ruling circle is guided by any specific set of considerations in its decision to keep holding elections in Russia. Acquiring popular legitimacy by presenting their rule as a reflection of the will of the people expressed through free elections is, undoubtedly, one important incentive to keep having them. It is just as evident that such legitimacy is important not only for domestic but also for international consumption. At least some in the ruling circle consider it important to maintain contacts with the outside world and, more precisely, with its most advanced countries, and a formal legitimation of one's rule through elections is a substantial precondition for maintaining relationships with those governments.

The staying power of established procedures is apparently an additional factor. Once elections have become part of the existing political system, it is easier, psychologically and for other reasons, to adapt them to the system's needs than to abolish them altogether. Yet the essential point is that, within the framework of such a system, the institution of elections will function only as long as the system is able to control their outcome. The failure to do so will mean either that the authoritarian system is collapsing or that the decision will be made to eliminate elections from the system's institutional machinery.

Of course, members of the ruling circle view occasional, localized failures (from their point of view) of control over the outcomes of elections as possible and tolerable. Usually, these failures later get fixed. For instance, in Yaroslavl's mayoral elections of 2012, Yevgeny Urlashov, a candidate who was inconvenient for the authorities, was elected, but he was arrested shortly afterwards on corruption charges and removed from office. One can also think of borderline situations, so to speak, in which the authorities allow fairly broad political competition so as to create an illusion of expanding it, with the possibility that this expansion will become irreversible.

Yet, overall, they want the mechanism to work well and to preclude any unplanned outcomes. If, in spite of all the efforts and measures taken to prevent them, the failures of the election machinery to produce expected outcomes exceed a certain threshold of what is tolerable for the authorities, then either the system itself will be transformed or, much more likely, the ruling circle will jettison the institution of elections in favor of more user-friendly tools of governance.

RENT EXTRACTION BY GOVERNMENT BUREAUCRACY

A system of governance like the one in Russia plainly does not contain within itself any goals, except for its inherent goal of perpetuating itself over time. Within this system of governance, the goals and meaningful content are set by the ruling circle, in accordance with the value orientations shared by the majority of its members. Thus, one cannot claim that an authoritarian system is invariably just a vehicle for personal enrichment of the people in power, or an instrument of suppressing individual freedoms, or, alternatively, a modernizing and developmental tool. As with most phenomena of practical social reality, authoritarianism cannot be universally defined by a single purpose. Everything depends on the context of a particular time and place, on the qualities of the elites, on the individual characteristics of the leaders at the top, and so on.

Yet any authoritarian system also has a feature that is absent from any system that is unequivocally competition-based: authoritarianism enables the ruling circle to extract administrative rent from their monopolistic grip on power. Due to their sole ownership of political resources in the country, the ruling circle has the opportunity to set up, at their complete discretion and without being held accountable for it, their own rewards and perks of all kinds, both formal and informal, individual and collective, for discharging their administrative functions. These rewards may be tied to performing specific governance-related activities or may be completely detached from them and thus simply serve as a bonus accruing to the powers that be, due to their position in society. The revenues extracted by members of the ruling circle may derive merely from its monopoly on violence and the resulting opportunities to practice outright extortion. This applies, for example, to uniformed agencies.

In an authoritarian system, there is no other power that is even able to fully determine the amounts, the forms, and the channels of these rent revenues accruing to the ruling circle, let alone to put a restraint on their indulgence and voracity. Essentially, this is the central weakness of authoritarian systems: with no built-in devices to limit the rulers' wants, sooner or later these systems become powerless to contain the tidal wave of selfishness, avarice, and social irresponsibility of the ruling group members.

History tells us that the idea of a competition-based political system, with the spread of the sources of power among different elite groups, separate branches of power, and systems of checks and balances, was ultimately rooted in a fundamental philosophical assessment of human nature. This assessment, developed over many centuries of historical experience, presumes that no individual is solely and permanently guided by one's ideals and the laws; that every human is fallible, prone to greed, vanity, and the pursuit of power; that one is uncritical of one's own behavior and misperceives other people's motivations and the outcomes of their activities. And being in power accentuates the failings and the vices even of people who have extensive experience and an excellent professional background. This is precisely why, over the long haul, only restrictions upon one's personal power allow a government to maintain its effectiveness, to make sure it reflects broadly shared interests, and to prevent or limit the extent of power abuse. One of the famous slogans of the Soviet era claimed that one's conscience is his best keeper. In contrast, the founding fathers of democracies in the world proceeded from the assumption that only external controls and a distribution of governmental functions across as many agencies as possible in a state can minimize the actual power abuse that is driven by the cravings and selfishness of individual power holders. This can be fully rendered by a Russian saying that has been very well understood in the United States: "Trust, but verify."

If, at some time in the past, authoritarianism in Russia experienced periods of voluntary moderation and self-restraint without a commensurate pressure from below, it has by now ostensibly outgrown these internally imposed limitations. As, also is noted by the scholar Daron Acemoglu, at this stage of a nation's maturity, the threat of social upheaval, of a revolution, becomes the only reason for the elite to restrain themselves.[3] If such a threat is not acute or immediate, or at least is not perceived as such by the authorities, it cannot act as a brake on their behavior; hence, they keep extracting administrative rents from the rest of the population on an ever larger scale. Strictly speaking, there is no way to measure the amount of this rent with precision; all those prominent economists who lay claims to discoveries in this regard are just trying to mislead the public, to put it mildly. If there is any proof of the increase in the scale of this transfer of wealth, it is localized and anecdotal. Nevertheless, all direct and indirect evidence indicates that, in Russia in the second decade of the twenty-first century, this rent extraction is ongoing and even blooming.

Thus, all the major costs of economic activities in Russia (the cost of labor, the cost of energy, transportation costs, administrative burdens, real estate rents, security costs, and so on) have been rapidly increasing since the turn of the century, with the exception of a brief period during the 2008–2009 global financial crisis. The capacity of the federal budget to provide investments in public infrastructure are diminishing and their efficiency is conspicuously declining. The quality of infrastructure work is going down, even on projects that have been a high priority for the Kremlin because of their public nature and geopolitical significance, such as the Asia-Pacific Economic Cooperation summit in Vladivostok or the Olympic Games in Sochi.

Government economic initiatives, such as the project to establish financial "development agencies," government-owned corporations in innovation-oriented industries, special economic zones, and many other ideas that were presented as emblematic of government intentions, have either been quietly shelved or, worse, have become the source of recurrent bad news. The undertakings and the projects that had been portrayed by Russian authorities as seminal have now become the target of their most stringent public critique. And, increasingly, economic decisions made by the government get suspended after an extended period of time since their adoption and after large expenditures toward their implementation have already been incurred.

All of this, taken together, strongly indicates that members of the ruling circle are becoming increasingly open about their focus upon vigorous appropriation of administrative rent, and this makes it less and less likely that they will accomplish any long-term tasks that require an expanded time horizon for planning and organizing implementation and oversight. And this is so even though, unlike in a competition-based system, the authoritarian system is not burdened by the electoral cycles that, objectively speaking, impede long-term planning because of the inherently short-term interests and motivations associated with them.

At the same time, however counterintuitive it may sound, such a decline in the efficiency of governance and abandonment of long-term visions indirectly indicate that post-Soviet authoritarianism in Russia has entered a mature neo-totalitarian stage. At this stage, all the essential features of an authoritarian system have already shown up and are now taking their more or less final shape. This suggests that the authoritarian regime has already subdued all those internal strivings and intents that were not coming from its core and that were associated with the personal aspirations and illusions of post-Soviet leaders. At this point, the objectively existing patterns and characteristics of this form of political organization of society are coming to the fore. And these characteristics are such that any active developmental ambition of an authoritarian system entirely depends on the individual motivations and energy of its leaders; the system contains within it no built-in automatic mechanisms that would propel it toward modernization.

With regard to the individual motivations of political leaders and the energy required to make these motivations work, the biological aspect of human nature leaves only a short time span in history during which leaders can play any role. Given the lack of turnover in government, which is one of the essential features of authoritarianism, the unavoidable result is the rotting of authoritarian regimes. That is, Russia's interest in reaching certain goals that are meaningful for the nation as a whole yields fairly quickly to the ruling circle's one-sided focusupon the acquisition and the divvying up of "legitimate spoils"—administrative rents.

IN SEARCH OF AN IDEOLOGY

The typical authoritarian political model as we know it from history has several systemic features. One feature that plays a significant role is the fuzziness of its ideological underpinnings. This is mainly due to authoritarian systems' interstitial positioning between, on the one hand, competition-based systems, in which ideology is actively employed to differentiate among political groups competing among themselves for the right of temporary access to the levers of governance, and, on the other hand, totalitarian systems, which use rigid dogmas of a particular totalitarian ideology as a tool for winning and maintaining power.

Totalitarian systems need an ideology in the form of a set of ideas and beliefs intended to be implanted into the consciousness of every individual and into society as a whole as the only valid set of views about the world. Such an ideology serves as a potent tool of political control over society, used to galvanize its members for action and to mobilize them in defense of the system when necessary. Totalitarianism always and everywhere relies first and foremost upon organized coercion applied to society by the powers that be. But such violence cannot be the sole basis of its power because it cannot provide strong enough cohesion to society without at the same time brainwashing people to instill in them the ideological motivations to act in the ways expected by the system and its leaders. Hence the need for "the only true teaching," with its concomitant rituals, cults, and role models, as well as the tireless and perpetual fight against this teaching's enemies, whether open, hidden, or even potential.

But competition-based political systems also call for ideological underpinnings. They are needed for the system as a whole, for its basic principles and general structure, and we can therefore think of democracy itself as an ideology. Ideology is also needed by the individual competing groups that are vying with each other, at least pro forma, not as clans built around the shared personal interests of their members but as like-minded people voicing shared beliefs about what makes a just and effective form of politics. In turn, these beliefs are most often at least superficially bound together by a certain system of views about the proper or fair organization of society—which is essentially what we call an ideology.[4] This is exactly why competition-based political systems tend to include a rather diverse spectrum of ideologies, even though the interests of the system's survival compel it to keep this diversity within certain boundaries—which means, in particular, suppressing various totalitarian ideologies, including religious currents with a totalitarian bent.

Meanwhile, authoritarian systems, positioned in the middle between totalitarian and competition-based systems, tend to be rather colorless, in ideological terms. Within the framework of such a system, the authorities usually do not pursue total control over citizens' minds and do not try to impose upon them uniform views about social and political developments. Sometimes such self-restraint is the conscious choice of the rulers and sometimes it is due to the lack of necessary resources. Either way, an authoritarian state does not pursue such goals and instead limits itself to controlling financial resources as well as administrative and coercive power.

Given that such control is quite sufficient for the authorities to safeguard themselves and to perpetuate their power, they pay scant attention to ideology and to what goes on in people's hearts and minds. And since an authoritarian power does not seek to instill ideological uniformity, it tends to permit the existence of various currents of thought in society, public debates among them, and even "soft" forms of organizing among like-minded individuals. This organizing is allowed as long as it does not lead to the emergence of political organizations possessing large amounts of resources and capable of claiming power in society and government. Moreover, objectively speaking, ideological debates in society turn out to benefit the authoritarian government because such debates prevent those unhappy with the government from unifying within a single camp, due to the conspicuous ideological differences among the forces interested in bringing the current power system down. And the broader the ideological spectrum, the less likely it is that the opposition groups will coordinate their activities with one another.

Although the autocratic rulers themselves usually try to project some ideological power, they are not good at that; they are not making the effort, they are not enthusiastic, and they usually do not achieve any lasting results. In such a system, government agencies are staffed with individuals selected according to the convenience of working with them and the opportunities to extract revenues in the form of administrative rent. Although the system undoubtedly requires them to display outer loyalty, it usually does not impose any particular demands upon their mind-set or views. Thus, because the characteristics required for comfortably operating within the system are distributed among people according to the laws of nature and do not closely correlate with their ideological preferences, the resulting composition of government staff tends to be rather diverse, in ideological terms.

And even though the ruling corporate circle unquestionably projects certain ideological messaging for public consumption (typically emphasizing patriotism and deep-rooted values), it is devoid of internal cohesion. Unless an authoritarian system morphs into a totalitarian one, it remains an eclectic assortment of individuals who are ideologically and even culturally quite different from one another. Accordingly, every attempt to produce an ideology that would bring everyone together ends with a standard menu of trivial statements against the backdrop of everyone's blatant hypocrisy.

This feature of authoritarianism fully manifested itself in Russia's political system of the first decade of the twenty-first century. In the 1990s, when authoritarian rule was beginning to take shape and when the abandonment of a competition-based political system as a lodestar for post-Soviet Russia was not yet so obvious, the ruling circle tried to differentiate itself ideologically from those groups that it was promoting into the role of the opposition; the authorities were actively trying to play the ideological role of the "reformers." This was made simpler by the fuzziness of the goals that were officially proclaimed as the direction of government work and that were overwhelmingly shared by the ruling circle. These goals included transition to the market, development of private ownership, loosening of restrictions on contacts with the West, recognition of ideological pluralism, and so on. The obvious difference between these goals and the foundational principles of the Soviet era enabled individual authorities to distinguish themselves through rhetoric about things like the "policies of reform" or the "reformist spirit."

In the first decade of the new century, however, the situation changed. On the one hand, the socioeconomic inequality that became rampant in the 1990s and, most of all, the illusory character of the notion of mass-scale private entrepreneurship as a means of raising Russians' incomes drastically reduced the appeal of the ideology of "market reforms."[5] On the other hand, societal fatigue from the uncertainties and inconveniences associated with the drastic changes in the social and professional organization of society in the 1990s generated popular demand for stability and predictability. This was further reinforced by the mass disenchantment with every kind of rhetoric; whereas in the 1980s many Russians had viewed freedom of speech as a key to progress, by now it turned out that free speech per se provided neither tangible goods nor genuine changes in the life of society. Thus, in the first few years of the twenty-first century, as the authoritarian rule was consolidating and becoming aware of its power and maturity, its ideological persona was becoming less and less distinctive.

For example, the rhetoric of market reforms and the anticommunist fervor of the mid-1990s have disappeared from government officials' speeches and pronouncements. References to their commitments to democratic values and to upholding political rights and freedoms also gradually receded into the background. At the same time, while official rhetoric now includes a tinge of nostalgia for Soviet times, it has led to neither a restoration of Marxism as the state ideology nor a clear shift toward a Western European–style leftist socialist ideology. Instead, Russia's newly minted authorities were more inclined to portray themselves as centrists, committed to practical constructive work and real-life concerns that reflected the interests of the people (in contrast to the "chatterboxes" of the opposition). Such an ideological posture enabled the ruling circle to recruit people of widely ranging ideological leanings and a variety of political backgrounds. It also provided the requisite flexibility to engage a broad spectrum of relevant groups and strata of society without completely alienating any large, influential circles of professional people.

The beginning of the rapid rise of Russians' incomes and of the financial capacity of the state at the start of the twenty-first century was another contributing factor. It enabled the ruling circle to instill in society optimism about its future and to distribute various handouts in exchange for recipients' reluctant acceptance of the government, without demanding of them a uniformity of ideological views. In a certain sense, the ideological passivity of the Kremlin in the mid-aughts indicated the strength of its position. As the volume of financial transactions in the country grew, and while the authorities had the power to control these flows, it was unnecessary to look for an additional ideological means to bind people to the authorities and ensure their self-perpetuation in power. The Kremlin was too confident and at ease with the situation to step upon the slippery slope of the quest for some official ideology; instead, it opted for the vague and eclectic rhetoric of just "working for the benefit of the people and the country." Only by the end of the aughts did it become evident that the period of nearly automatic rapid growth of incomes was coming to an end (it was simply too good to be true for too long, for objective reasons) and that the opportunities for the appropriation and distribution of administrative rents had hit their limits. It was then that the ruling circle became conspicuously more active in its pursuit of additional ideology to prop itself up.

An additional impetus for this pursuit was that the decrease in economic opportunities caused by the petering out of income growth coincided with the election cycle of 2011–2012. In a system in which elections are essentially an extraneous element, an implant from another political model, the mere holding of elections, with the inevitable campaign agitation by every political force, generates additional tension within the system, regardless of the authorities' confidence about their position and their control over the outcome of the elections. In addition, the rising pitch of political debates, which previously had been rather listless, now had the potential to influence the minds of the masses in ways that were undesirable for the authorities. The intensity of these debates could possibly awaken faint rumblings under the surface of society, and soon, in an unexpected situation, people might be ready to support so-called extremists capable of undermining government control over the situation in the country.

Given all this, in the early 2010s, Russia's authorities became noticeably more interested in developing a more distinctive ideological stance. The direction of this quest emerged spontaneously and pointed toward a conservative, status quo ideology of defending the authorities as the only personification of Russia's national interest and of resisting all political change. This is the direct reason for all those ideological trends that were plain to see after 2010 and that we continue to observe today. Let me enumerate the most prominent among them.

First, the Russian government engaged in relentless propagandizing of the need for "strong power." In this framework, "strong" means not so much effective or capable of maintaining law and order; rather, it means a power that is not to be questioned, that is untouchable and has some mystical underpinning equating it with statehood and nationhood as a whole.[6] In this new framework, the state is not just equal to the powers that be; it is a function of their activities. So an assault upon the ruling circle is viewed as an attempt to destroy the state itself. Essentially, the Kremlin has taken up the idea of autocracy—not as it was known in the Romanovs' imperial Russia but in the meaning that it takes in political Eurasianism. This involves a deification of power as sacred in itself and not accountable to any institutions. It is presented as allegedly the natural and sole form of existence of Russia's statehood and the only one that safeguards Russia against extreme polarization and the fragmentation of society.

Officially, the system holds on to elections as a form of legitimation of the country's supreme authorities. Yet, ideologically, elections are presented not as an opportunity to select one of several candidates competing with one another on an equal basis but as a selfless, heroic struggle of Vladimir Putin, the sole and unrivalled tsar and leader of the nation, against presumptuous attempts by outsiders, impostors, to take the throne away from its legitimate holder. Hence the conspicuous absence of the "Chief Candidate" from presidential debates (since the autocrat cannot bring himself down to the level of personal debate with impostors); hence the aura of majestic grandeur in government media's presentation of this candidate; hence the emphatic support from senior clergy of Russia's top religion, the Orthodox Church of the Moscow Patriarchate. In this framework, elections of the chief of state turn into an expression of the people's support for the authorities—which meets everyone's expectations and is encouraged through a variety of means. This demonstration of support is based not on a hardheaded assessment of the quality of governance and the resulting quality of life but rather on the notion of defending the powers that be, as the personification of the state, against their weakening, whether willful or accidental, by various "schismatics."

The second ideological trend, resulting naturally from the first, is that supporting the authorities is portrayed as the civic duty of the people in its entirety, regardless of the extent of disagreements among them. Accordingly, if someone refuses to support the authorities, let alone rebels against them, this indicates, whether directly or indirectly, that its opponents are not a part of the Russian people. The media and the government present such behavior, at best, as an honest blunder under the influence of various harmful ideas and, at worst, as a consequence of not loving one's people, not understanding their interest, or deliberately betraying them.

In the past few years, this theme has become particularly pronounced. The presentation of all opponents of the ruling circle as antisocial, hostile to the Russian people, belonging to some other, non-Russian society has become one of the key messages of the political and ideological broadcasting by the main government-owned media. Moreover, the point that is hammered over and over again is that all opponents and adversaries of the present authorities represent a fifth column directed from abroad with the aim of dismantling Russia's statehood, causing the breakup and partition of the country, enslaving its people, and so on. This ideological trick solves two primary tasks: on the one hand, it deprives those in the opposition who advocate for a European path for Russia of a mass following; on the other, it constrains those who call themselves a patriotic opposition by undermining their political base and pushing them to the fringe, as they face the choice between endorsing the powers that be or being labeled extremists who must be kept away from the levers of government power.

Finally, the third ideological tenet posits a hostile international environment. As a matter of fact, this logically complements the first and second propositions. Indeed, a ruling circle that is the sole embodiment of the notion of Russia's statehood and peoplehood must resist those hostile forces that seek to ruin and destroy this statehood. Accordingly, if all the parts and strata of the people are rallying around this ruling circle, it means that the state's enemies are somewhere outside of the country, an external enemy and a threat to the nation. This naturally leads to an increasingly emphatic anti-American and, more broadly, anti-Western outlook, transmitted by the ruling circle to the public, with finger-pointing at the West and especially at the United States as the eternal and irreconcilable foe of Russian statehood.

The propagandistic portrayal of the West as the main and virtually the only foreign enemy of the nation logically flows from the Russian establishment's favorite message, wherein those who criticize the Russian government are against the Russian people and are influenced from abroad. There is virtually no other candidate for this role of chief villain—although, were the Kremlin propaganda in a certain sense more forthright and less cowardly, it might discern a primordial challenge to itself in the unsettlingly rapid rise of China or in the methodical spread of a radical, militant strand of political Islam.

Nonetheless, for various reasons, the West has turned out to be the most convenient for Russia to portray as the primary threat and adversary. On the one hand, the West is more laid back than China or the aggressive wing of political Islam in responding to confrontational rhetoric; as a rule, its response is also merely rhetorical. Essentially, the West has accepted the rules of Russia's political postmodernism, which leaves enough room for publicly calling the Western establishment the enemy of Russian statehood while, at the same time, demanding from this establishment visa-free travel and promotion of trade and investment in Russia. Meanwhile, Russia's ruling circle is well aware that an attempt to play such a game with China (let alone trying, for example, to establish Russian control over China's internal distribution networks) would be immediately and abruptly blocked by the Chinese.

On the other hand, the aggregate image of the West is a natural common enemy for a panoply of different currents and forces inside Russia that espouse an idealistic view of "traditional" society and set it up against the present-day postindustrial society, which they see as "corrupted" by "virulent" forces of liberalism.[7] The power of the negative image of the West to mobilize public outrage in Russia is notably higher than the potential power of the negative image of any alternative candidates for the role of Russia's chief external foe.

Finally, as the most powerful force in today's world, the West as adversary suits the aspirations of the Russian elite, who, since the Soviet era, have become accustomed to viewing themselves as central on the global stage. In spite of the increase in the relative importance of former Third World countries in global politics, Russians and their elite do not view any one of them, including China, or even all of them taken together, as a worthy adversary for the former superpower. In addition, the present authoritarian regime views the United States and Western Europe as the only political players in the world with reason and means, however limited, to bolster the forces inside Russia that could fully or partially escape from this regime's control. From the point of view of the ruling circle, no other global players have either the requisite means or a sufficiently strong desire to do so.

Granted, direct Western support for civic organizations in Russia oriented toward European political culture has been relatively insignificant, and Western rhetorical assessments of Russia's political system have been rather bland. Even so, given the many historical commonalities between the peoples of Russia and of the European Union, if Western rhetorical challenges psychologically resonate with Russia's mass consciousness at some point in the future, then Russia's post-Soviet system may experience a major ideological crisis, if not an outright collapse. The many examples of peaceful "color revolutions" since the turn of the century, as well as similar confrontations that ended up in government use of force, do not look like something that could be easily transplanted onto Russian soil. But that is today, and what may happen tomorrow causes considerable, even if somewhat irrational, fear among Russia's present-day rulers.

Thus, the view of the United States and NATO as enemies and chief potential adversaries is convenient for the authorities from the standpoint of ideological struggle against the opposition, while at the same time it reflects real concerns of the ruling circle with regard to the West's interference in matters that the Kremlin views as nobody else's business. Either way, anti-Western rhetoric has become an important component of the ideological identity of Russia's authoritarian regime. It would be erroneous to dismiss it as a short-term response or as merely a convenient tool for accomplishing immediate tasks.

The fourth ideological trend is that the government and its media are increasingly pumping up Russians' sense of pride and self-esteem. In principle, this is nothing unusual and is entirely normal. The civil society of any country has a natural need for a collective sense of self-esteem, which is built up using historical events (such as military victories and conquests), economic successes, achievements in sports, and many other elements. Invoking past and present national success stories does not constitute any kind of ideology per se. However, an ideological twist appears whenever these achievements start to be used as justification for the lack of normal living standards, the lack of functioning public institutions or their failure to perform, or the lack of clarity about the vision of the future development of the country and its people (as in, "We don't have any of that, but we are making missiles instead").

Of course, the boundary between the typical self-confidence of a nation and a propagandistic twist to such confidence is not set in stone, but it is easy to discern when government and the media overstep that boundary. This happens, for example, when they start exploiting history as a source of newly created myths extended into the present and the future and allegedly demonstrating the country's "special role" or its mystical "manifest destiny" as the guide for other nations. This happens when government enacts laws that penalize skepticism about the country's historic achievements or the special historic mission of its people. It also happens when the authorities give sports tournaments a political, government-level status, linking athletes' victories to the political course of the government and the ruling party and exploiting them to promote the ruling circle. (Those who grew up in Soviet times should be very familiar with all this.)

Has this boundary between Russia's national self-confidence and its propagandistic distortion already been crossed? As of this writing, my sense is that we are there. And it is being done in an ever outrageous manner.

Finally, a fairly important ingredient of the regime's new ideology has been its reliance upon propaganda about the so-called traditional, premodern beliefs of such institutions as the family, the church, and the nation-state. All this is done in a very Eurasianist style; that is, Marxist–Leninist ideas about society, seen as having lost their efficacy, are replaced with "tradition"—family tradition, religious tradition, or government tradition. Of course, this is done through an entirely superficial and historically flawed interpretation. In its intensity as well as its ignorance and unscrupulousness, this ideological work is on a par with the worst examples of totalitarian propaganda.

This trend is exemplified by the authorities' and the media's confrontational stance toward minorities of all kinds—by granting government functions to religion and the church and by the tendency to impart an ethnic-based identity to the state, solidifying, ideologically and politically, the status of ethnic Russians as the core "indigenous" ethnicity (so far, however, without formalizing this in legal terms). In this regard, the new ideology of authoritarianism in Russia is clearly an about-face on Soviet-era ideology. The new ideology fits in with its Soviet predecessor with regard to the four aspects that I mentioned earlier: viewing the powers that be as a given that is not subject to questioning, labeling dissenters as enemies of the people and outcasts, positing a powerful and hostile encirclement by foreign enemies, and inflating the sense of national pride as a substitute for the normal functioning of public institutions, though this final aspect is largely negated by reverting to the legacy of pre-Soviet Russia.

With regard to ethnicity, however, the rhetorical difference between Putin's Russia and the late Soviet period is rather stark. Even though, in practice, Soviet authorities assumed the primacy of Russian language and culture and the need for tight political control over ethnic minorities, it nevertheless formally based itself upon the tenet of equality among cultures (an analog to the European notion of multiculturalism) and the need to integrate the country's ethnicities into some sort of a cohesive community of Soviet people. Consequently, Soviet authorities were resolute in cracking down on public displays of hate speech against any ethnicity—even though there were in fact implicit quotas on the representation of various ethnic groups in government, in uniformed agencies, and in the "politically sensitive" fields of culture, education, and applied science. In the late Soviet period, it would be unthinkable to have government-owned television giving a platform to someone who calls for "kicking migrants out of Moscow," meaning in fact all those who do not look like ethnic Russians, or for knocking some ethnic minorities "under the pavement"—the kinds of statements that can be found in the official media today. In the Soviet period, coercive government agencies used all of their power to suppress any attempts by anyone to launch pogroms out of the blue—the kind of violence that today gets public approval and encouragement from establishment figures and even government officials.

The issue of policies toward minorities that are not connected to a specific territory is rather tricky. Like any other totalitarian ideology, the Soviet belief system assumed the need to impose on all its subjects a uniform set of views about the world; in this sense, the notion of protecting minority rights was completely alien to it. Nevertheless, it implicitly acknowledged the differences among people, whether given or historically conditioned, with regard to their ethnic and class origins, cultural affinities, and so on. Soviet authorities did not recognize the right of minorities to emphasize their identity in public. Back then, a Jewish congress or a Cossack legion or a gay pride organization would have been unthinkable. And, in practice, some of these minorities were being suppressed or restricted. However, after Joseph Stalin's death, in 1953, the Soviet regime did not tolerate any attempts to publicly denounce and victimize ethnic and cultural minorities, at least as long as such groups stayed within the limits of behavior that were imposed on them.

In contrast, in the new realities of post-Soviet Russia, minorities face a terrible choice: either fit into the system within the confines of the roles assigned to them and according to their willingness to perform these roles, or be a target of government-sanctioned attacks. It is worth noting that the purpose of such public attacks is not to physically evict minorities from Russia's public space (or at least this is not yet the purpose) but rather to give nonminority Russians a sense of their superiority over at least some of their compatriots while, at the same time, letting the steam of their pent-up anger out of the kettle.

Clearly, this facet of the regime's authoritarian ideology will become increasingly pronounced and rigid with the rise of the levels of anger in society—and these levels may keep rising, due to economic difficulties, changes in ethnic demography in specific territories and in the "politically sensitive" fields of economic activity, and the disorganization of everyday life caused by the growth of corruption and the overall weakness of governance. The resulting increase in hostility toward minorities will affect the content of mass media broadcasting, which will assume an increasingly imperial tenor in terms of enforcing a rigid hierarchy of values and the groups that embody them. This also will influence actual policies, which will be increasingly geared toward inciting hatred for ideological as well as various ethnic and cultural minorities.

And yet, going back to the beginning of this section, it must be noted that the ever more pronounced ideological twist of the Putin regime in recent years, and its attempts to secure a wider base through more intensive brainwashing of the public, suggest that the system has already passed the peak of its resilience.[8] The growing rebelliousness in society, engulfing primarily its most active parts, has increased to the point where the ruling circle feels its presence, and feels it so sharply, that its prior confidence about controlling the situation without ideological props, in a relatively comfortable and secure manner, is rapidly beginning to evaporate.

As a matter of fact, the Kremlin's new strategy, based on emphasizing the regime's ideological persona, is much riskier than its prior approach, as it awakens and mobilizes the potentially destructive elements in society. The ruling circle clearly expects to be able to keep these elements under control and to use them exclusively against its opponents. However, controlling destructive forces of nature is a very complicated task. To assume that these blind forces will not erupt and destroy society itself, with its tricky and fragile system of balances, means accepting huge risks at best. At worst, the rulers risk being liable for the disastrous consequences of a false confidence in the government's powers of control.

CORRUPTION AS A SYSTEM

The system of governance that has taken shape in Russia is not just an authoritarian regime. It is a system functioning within the distinctive conditions of the transformation of the Soviet system (which degenerated and thus failed to meet the challenges of its time) into capitalism of a peripheral type. This is a capitalism that has no internal sources for its growth and is functioning on the fringe of the global market economy.

These conditions have inevitably imparted some peculiar features to Russia's authoritarianism. The first among these characteristics is certainly the exorbitant level of corruption that is endemic to the system. In principle, corruption exists everywhere. To some extent, it affects every highly organized society. Moreover, the higher the level of a society's organization, the larger is the element of corruption—if understood not in the narrow sense, as primitive bribe-taking, but more broadly, as including conflicts of interests among government officials, the practice of taking advantage of insider information, deliberate promotion and servicing of private interests in government, and so on. Likewise, a number of borderline phenomena characteristic of a developed society also can be viewed as a form of corruption in this broad sense of the term. These include the practice of legislators' advocacy of the interests of their campaign donors, or elected officials' sharing of information with "their" media and consultants. Thus, when we say that Russia's political system and its analogs in other countries are characterized by systemic corruption, what is distinctive here is not the presence of corruption per se but rather its large scale and its many forms, or, more precisely, the special role played by corruption in the functioning of the system in its entirety.

Of course, the forms of corruption that are observed in present-day Russia are not unique to it and are fully in line with those that are known from elsewhere; they are described a thousand times in academic and general-audience writings and even in fiction. Naturally, at the lowest layers of governance, where agencies handle relatively small amounts of resources, the more primitive forms of corruption are more prevalent. These include trivial theft and bribery, kickbacks to officials for contracting with public procurement funds, and procuring from firms that belong—directly or indirectly, fully or in part—to those who allocate and manage these public contracts. These forms of corruption certainly do exist at the higher levels of bureaucracy. However, at that level they also are supplemented with more intricate forms, such as administrative protection for one's own family business and securing preferential conditions for it; building sophisticated networks of family relationships and friendships aimed at taking personal advantage of one's high-level government status; tricky, multilayered mechanisms of extortion from private businesses; and so on.

At the same time, in the case of Russia, the underdevelopment and extreme vulnerability of social and economic institutions under the peripheral type of capitalism have shaped two distinctive features that set its corruption apart from the type that exists in the countries belonging to the core of the world capitalist system:

1. the relative underdevelopment of sophisticated and veiled forms of corruption that require a higher-level institutional structure for their implementation; and
2. a more explicit relationship between corruption-driven enrichment and the outflows of capital from Russia.

The country's comparatively unsophisticated corruption is a predictable consequence of the underdevelopment of large private businesses and the institutions servicing their needs. Indeed, the stock market, which serves as a major tool of corrupt enrichment, using confidential insider information available to high-ranking government officials, plays a very limited role in Russia's economy. Its trading volume, as well as the range and complexity of its financial instruments, are meager compared to those in global financial centers. Accordingly, there are rather limited gains to be made from using insider information to enrich oneself through stock market operations or other transactions involving financial assets whose value might be predicted based on classified information.

Likewise, the opportunities for private business interests in Russia to lobby for legislation are rather insignificant. One reason for this is that legislative bodies cannot introduce any significant legislation on their own, without the executive authorities. The second reason is that, in general, in a peripheral type of capitalism, the law plays a very limited role in determining the actual parameters of business operations and the distribution of their gains. Under these circumstances, expenditures toward legislative lobbying are unlikely to pay off either in the medium term or in the long term. In addition, using private business resources to secure elected positions in present-day Russia is rather difficult, both because elections are controlled by the authoritarian "power vertical" and because very few elected positions confer any real power and freedom of action in the first place.

On top of this, the distribution of financial flows in this economic reality is so tightly intertwined with government power that it simply does not leave any room for truly complex and multistage forms of influence. That is, those who do not have access to the vertical hierarchy of power have no real means to influence the direction of financial flows in any substantial way. Meanwhile, those who are included in this vertical have no need to complicate the process of taking advantage of their access to financial flows; their appointment in and of itself is viewed by all as an invitation to the party, which includes an implicit mandate for personal enrichment by quite overt, simple, and unsophisticated means.

The second distinctive feature of corruption in Russia, its close connection with the export of capital, is also conditioned by a number of interrelated factors. First, the opportunities for investing corruption-generated revenue inside Russia are limited by high risks. As the volume of such domestic investment grows, these risks increase as well. Under the present system, if the owner of these investments cannot personally manage this capital as a business enterprise, the chances of losing the monies earned by one's "hard work" and transferred to someone else's care are unacceptably high.

In addition to the risks involved, the peripheral character of Russia's capitalism objectively limits productive utilization of new capital. Russia's main industry—the production and export of oil, gas, and other natural resources—is dominated by a group of big firms, with virtually no entry point for newcomers, especially those with private funds. Manufacturing is viable in only a limited number of areas. And almost all successful high-tech ventures eventually force their owners—in most cases, due to objective factors—to move the business away from Russia and into the intellectual, technological, and organizational space of modern economies of the global core elsewhere in the world. Thus, those who are engaged in corruption-driven primitive accumulation of capital and plan to benefit from it in the future typically invest in foreign assets (primarily real estate or the launch and development of some kind of family business abroad). This represents a significant share of capital outflows from Russia.

Another factor that links corruption to the export of capital is that, as the stratum of rich or just very affluent Russians emerges and expands, their yearning for full integration into the global elite, focused around the so-called West, is growing and will continue to grow. This is yet another consequence of Russian capitalism's peripheral position. This trend is a given and it is irreversible. Under globalization, children of successful elites from every region of the developing world—from India to Africa to Latin America—acquire property in the United States and Western Europe and park there a large part of their family assets. This goes on in spite of the psychological resistance and even active rejection of the West in the minds of the first generation of wealthy elites; many of their members would rather maintain their cultural and physical independence from the Western world that is foreign and alien to them. But, with generational change, and in many cases even without it, the realities of managing massive amounts of wealth take over, and even powerful ideological barriers (such as political Islam in Arab countries) are powerless to contain these large assets and their owners in their places of origin.

It is therefore unsurprising that the Kremlin's widely advertised campaign to promote the "nationalization" of Russia's elites was limited from the outset and is lacking in drive and persistence. Unlike many other government initiatives (some even more inappropriate and senseless than this one), this campaign was the only one to face outright objections and effective opposition from among the elites from the outset. This reaction significantly tempered the initial enthusiasm of some pro-government public figures who had eagerly sought to be at the forefront of this campaign. Moreover, data on capital outflow for the year 2013 indicated that the measures taken to compel high-ranking officials to close their bank accounts abroad went hand in hand with an apparent increase in the rate of capital export from Russia. (Unfortunately, in the statistical data it is practically impossible to separate export of capital by Russian citizens from repatriation of assets from Russia by citizens of other countries; therefore, we can only operate with hypotheses that have a high probability of being true.)

Yet the most important feature of a peripheral-type corruption is not the forms that it takes but rather its scale. In spite of all the publicity around corruption scandals that from time to time shake the global capitalist core—the United States and countries of Western Europe—this corruption is notably still so-called upper-level corruption; it mainly involves high-ranking government officials taking advantage of their position for personal benefit. However, the corruption that we see in the West almost never expands to the agencies that these higher-level corrupt officials supervise, and it does not transform these agencies into criminal enterprises as such—that is, the agencies do not function as a result of an existing opportunity for corruption-derived gain and essentially for the sake of this gain.

Moreover, the very publicity around these scandals in the West is evidence that those societies and governments have within them the means to crack down on corrupt activities of the highest-ranking officials before they manage to pervert the agencies that they manage to such an extent that they cease to perform the requisite functions of governance. These internal checks on the extent of corruption may be based on competition among agencies and on the unwillingness of the members of the political class to let their colleagues (competitors) enrich themselves by violating the rules of this competition, but this is beside the point.

There is one key distinction between corruption that is still bearable and corruption that is irreparably destructive. Contrary to the widespread assumption, so-called everyday corruption destroys governance much faster and to a greater extent than its upper-level variety. This is because everyday corruption demonstrates that the authorities have lost control of the operation of government machinery, or at least of its key parts. Therefore, this type of corruption annihilates citizens' trust in government institutions in their entirety.

Indeed, normalcy in the everyday life of the people and in the operation of businesses depends upon the lower and the middle ranks of government agencies. And if these public servants perform their functions well, the fact that these agencies' top brass may pocket more than they are entitled to does not excessively disorganize everyday life in the country. If police are fighting crime, if tax agencies provide revenues to the government, if those in charge of holding government agencies accountable ensure compliance with the laws and regulations, and if public health-care providers and public-school teachers are treating people and teaching kids rather than extorting bribes and donations, then even significant power abuse in the highest echelons of the government is not so much of a catastrophe for the nation.

However, if upper-level abuses are not cut short by periodic investigations and tough punishment for those found guilty, then the rot of corruption quickly spreads along the entire hierarchy of government. Its agencies can easily morph from public institutions into criminal corporations whose only goal and reason for existence is the extraction and maximization of personal gain through their monopolistic control over specific aspects of everyday life in the country. Under these circumstances, the agencies either do not perform their stated functions at all or they do it only pro forma and in their "spare time," which is bound to impact the effectiveness of government in its entirety.

Under such circumstances, too, the character of the state itself is greatly altered. It changes from being an institution with a public purpose, irreducible to securing the well-being of the ruling circle or even of a wider circle of privileged groups and strata of society, into an institution that exclusively serves the goals and objectives of a specific group of people. In this case, no one any longer expects or demands in earnest that individual agencies perform any public service tasks. These agencies now have to do nothing but fulfill their obligations with regard to other, more powerful groups of individuals. Meanwhile, all of these agencies' resources in excess of those needed to fulfill these obligations are viewed as individuals' property, which they are free to use toward their private interests and at their discretion.

If, over the course of its historical development, a given society has produced a type of government that we can call modern—an institution serving the nation as a whole and undertaking tasks other than maintaining the dominance of one group of people, however numerous—then corruption, if allowed to overstep certain boundaries, throws the state back to a premodern version of itself. Such a premodern government is an aggregate sum of corporate units wielding administrative power and organized by territory, by industry, and sometimes by function. Each of these corporate units accomplishes the tasks related to its own survival and prosperity while also fulfilling certain obligations with regard to corporations possessing more resources and authority.

In today's world, this type of state typically precludes the country from being a part of the advanced core of the world economy and of global capitalism. Nevertheless, this type of state may exist for a long time on the periphery of the world economy without coming into an acute conflict with the objective needs of its peripheral economy or with the needs of a society whose condition corresponds to this kind of an economy.

Turning from our general points to the case of the present-day authoritarianism in Russia, I believe we can confidently state that, regardless of its distinctive country-specific features, we are witnessing the country's regression into precisely such a premodern state. And corruption plays a decisive role in this process. Tolerance for corruption on the part of the government and society has been a fixture across all stages of the building of post-Soviet capitalism. Yet this corruption also exhibits clear-cut dynamics in its development. These dynamics may not be very visible in the short term, but they are quite pronounced over the long haul, and it has already resulted in a long-term weakening in Russia's government agencies' performance of the basic functions of the modern-type state. These functions include, among other things, ensuring that organizations and individuals at least formally comply with the law, protecting citizens from abuse and violence, ensuring that parties to contracts and agreements fulfill their terms, and providing the necessary minimum of government services to the public free of charge. It is true that the continuing erosion of these governance functions has not yet resulted in actual and complete paralysis. Yet it is hard to ignore the overall trend, and its simple extrapolation into the not-so-distant future gives us a clear picture of what lies ahead.

Now let us digress for a moment. When discussing transition economies, proponents of the institutional approach often tend to justify corruption, at least in part, from a functional point of view—as an opportunity to reallocate resources from an old elite to the new while avoiding direct confrontation between the two. This approach portrays corruption not as a form of deviant behavior but as the divergence between earlier established norms and the current models of behavior shaped by the changes in the socioeconomic environment. According to the functionalists' logic, corruption will die off on its own as the tension between the two normative systems becomes less acute, with the new rules supplanting the old ones and the new elite replacing their predecessors.

Whatever the case, this kind of transition did not materialize in Russia at the turn of the twenty-first century. The outcome was quite different: corruption techniques have become the foundation of economic activities. They have overpowered the functioning of both market competition and government regulation. Although some view corruption-based economic activity as a feature of the transition to a market economy, in practice it has become institutionalized for the long haul.

With private business and government having become inseparable from each other, and with conflicts of interest becoming institutionalized, pervasive, and ubiquitous, corruption has become qualitatively different from being merely a deviation from the law and the rules. It is becoming both the rule and the natural norm of behavior. Corruption has been transforming the entirety of public consciousness and has resulted in the following paradox: laws are being intentionally enacted so that they can be broken. An individual who does not partake in corruption-related activities as a matter of principle is largely and often irrevocably cut off from the means of upward mobility and is at risk of not surviving in this economy. In fact, the success of an individual member of society is evaluated by others in terms of one's ability to break the law without getting caught, and, moreover, to maximize one's financial gain in the process. And this is not some kind of an irrational, archaic, traditionalist rejection of formal laws. To the contrary, it is the most rational behavior in this particular context. Such a corrupt mentality cannot be rectified through education or through expanding business and human contacts with the developed world.

The supreme powers in the country are not bothered by this corruption-based system. In fact, it works to their advantage. Government compels society to be its accomplice in crime, as everyone gets involved in it, whether on a regular basis or from time to time, or abets this crime by being a passive observer. Moreover, corruption becomes the most important tool of governing this political system. Since the scale of tolerated corruption makes it virtually pervasive, the ruling circle can keep almost the entire elite in a state of uncertainty and fear—by making exceptions or qualifications, by suddenly paying attention to or, to the contrary, turning away from evidence, and by selectively turning the law enforcement machinery on or off, depending on the individuals or groups of people in question.[9] Essentially, Russia's present-day political system is identical with corruption; its anticorruption campaigns are nothing but struggling with oneself—and the outcomes are rather predictably ineffective.

And yet, in concluding this section, let me reiterate an earlier point that some may find debatable: the scale and forms of corruption in the government and politics of today's Russia are not an unavoidable, natural product of its authoritarian system of governance. As I mentioned at the beginning of the book, autocracies do not have to imply stagnation and the decay of their countries; both in theory and in practice, there can be authoritarian regimes geared toward modernizing their societies (even if this happens infrequently). Even though they are limited in time and have no long-term future, at a certain stage, and especially in the catching-up phase of modernization, they may be able to successfully achieve the goals of closing the gaps that separate their country from those with whom they are catching up in economic growth.

Alas, it is increasingly plain to see that today's Russia is not an example of this. The growth of corruption is out of control. It is hard to prove with numbers but easy to experience in person, through active participation in Russia's political and economic developments or even by carefully observing them. This is the strongest evidence that Russian authoritarianism is of a stagnation-prone, peripheral, demodernizing variety. It anchors Russia in a certain position within the world's economic and political pecking order—a position that isn't exactly honorable and, most importantly, holds no bright promise for Russia's future.

THE SOCIAL BASE OF PUTIN'S POWER

Another important feature of a peripheral-type autocracy is the distinctive configuration of its social base of support. But before undertaking a description and analysis of this support, I have to make another digression. When speaking of "peripheral" authoritarianism, I am aware that, at this point in history, all countries ruled by authoritarian regimes are located, one way or another, on the periphery of global capitalism, whereas the political systems of the countries included in capitalism's core are currently functioning on the basis of political competition. Granted, the framework of this competition may differ from one time and place to another, but in none of these countries is there a truly monopolistic grip on power by a fairly small group of people, as is typical in autocracies. Perhaps in this sense one can say that, at least at this time, there is no other type of authoritarianism than the one that exists on the periphery of the world system.

And yet I believe that identifying peripheral authoritarianism as an autonomous phenomenon is worthwhile, in terms of analyzing its characteristics in Russia. There are at least two rationales for this. First, the concept of world periphery is fairly elastic and covers economies and societies that differ widely from one another in terms of their complexity and degrees of modernization. Coincidentally, those authors who use the term "peripheral economy" in their works point to significant differences in the economies and the social structures of the countries included in this category, and they introduce the notion of "semi-peripheral" countries and economies.[10]

Accordingly, individual countries with authoritarian or similar political systems, while being part of the overall world periphery, are positioned at considerably different places with regard to the core of the world economy. Thus, on the one hand, there are quite a few dictatorial regimes that are parasitizing on a primitive, often seminatural and monocultural economy in the countries that lag behind the leaders of modern capitalism at a distance of one or even two historical periods. On the other hand, many countries that have been in the process of making or have already completed their historic leap toward the core of industrial civilization and are positioned on its borderline continue to maintain political systems in which the principles of free political competition operate on a very limited basis, if at all. Specific examples may include Singapore, Indonesia, oil kingdoms in the Middle East, and, finally, mainland China, with its one-party system and tight control over political developments. In these countries, some form of political authoritarianism coexists with quite modern forms of entrepreneurship and with high levels of education among a significant part of society, which is also highly receptive to new technologically advanced business.

Another reason to analyze Russia in terms of peripheral authoritarianism is that the trajectory of the political systems of even the most developed countries of the world—from their emergence to their present-day, competition-based polities—passed through some form of autocratic rule. And the autocratic periods in their histories are not that far removed from our times. Thus, both Japan and South Korea made their leaps toward their present position as part of the "Western world" not so long ago by history's standards. In South Korea, this was done under conditions of the ruling group's quite severe crackdown on political opposition; in Japan, the authorities steadily marginalized the opposition by nonviolent means.

Let us also not forget that, just forty or fifty years ago, some of the countries in Southern Europe that have by now become full members of the European Union were ruled by authoritarian regimes. And even many of the countries that today represent the leadership of the Western world completely transitioned to competition-based systems of parliamentary governance not so long ago. Moreover, some scholars believe that the "irreversible" nature of this transition is merely a hypothesis rather than an unassailable fact and may yet be disproven by an unexpected turn of events.[11]

Clearly, the character of authoritarian regimes in such countries was or has been different—both in form and, much more importantly, in core features—from the character of regimes that we observe in the countries of the deep periphery. Therefore, I believe that, in this sense, identifying peripheral authoritarianism as a distinct category with its own peculiar set of features is meaningful in both political and academic terms.

As I mentioned earlier, one of the distinctive features of peripheral-type autocracies is a specific configuration of their social base. In societies that have a fairly sophisticated economic organization and have already made considerable strides in the direction of joining the core of the global capitalist system, political regimes have tended to rely upon the bureaucracy of uniformed agencies as well as upon large-scale private owners of capital. The latter group plays a subordinate yet also a privileged, in many ways autonomous, and, most importantly, highly active role in such a system. At the same time, these "advanced" authoritarian regimes tend to combine their favorite populist and pseudo-egalitarian rhetoric, their propaganda of social harmony and the shared responsibility of all strata and classes for their country's development, with barely any policy to address the socioeconomic needs of their people, very modest social safety net guarantees, and harsh labor laws.

In contrast, autocracies in the countries located far on the outskirts of global capitalism do not much trust their uniformed agencies; are more hostile toward the entrepreneurial stratum, seeking to subordinate it entirely to their administrative bureaucracy (which is likely to serve as their primary support group); and tend to rely upon a relatively broad layer of lower classes, presenting themselves as the defenders of their interests.

There is a certain kind of logic behind these differences. If an authoritarian regime is seriously pursuing rapid, high-quality economic growth (the kind of growth that brings the structure of society closer to its role models in the developed world), then it has no choice but to harness the energy of private initiative, in its most sophisticated and productive manifestations. Hence the need for closely cooperating with big business, for defending its interests vis-à-vis labor, while also curbing the pretensions and cravings of the government bureaucracy, which is capable of putting up huge barriers to the free development of private initiative. And the only potential mighty ally of the ruling group in achieving the task of restraining civilian bureaucracy is the bureaucracy of the uniformed agencies, which are capable of serving as a real counterweight to civilian bureaucrats.

The opposite is also true: a passive approach to the notion of a genuinely modernizing development, an acceptance of the dominance of the simplest, even primitive forms of economic and social relations, and massive use of straightforward, undisguised corruption as tool of societal and state governance compels the upper crust of peripheral autocracies to rely upon the natural carriers of these social phenomena—civilian bureaucracy and its clients as well as the lower classes of society.

In light of this, let us now turn to the analysis of these characteristics as they manifest themselves in the realities of today's Russia. Predictably, since about 2005 we have seen the indicators of Russia's post-Soviet peripheral and autocratic character becoming gradually yet conspicuously more pronounced. This is especially visible when comparing the period of its emergence in the 1990s with the present stage of its maturity.

During the initial period (stubbornly yet erroneously associated by many observers with political liberalism), Russia's authorities harbored some illusions about the possibility of ensuring rapid growth, founded on Russia's newfound capitalist base, to catch up with the developed powers. Accordingly, members of the ruling group at the time sought to establish their base of support among representatives of the relatively younger generation—energetic people who were looking to succeed quickly and who gave credence to the idea that the new social order offered them a unique chance to drastically change their lives for the better. These people hoped to become the core of Russia's future entrepreneurial estate; they were not looking for the ruling group to provide them with material support, a social safety net, or high-quality public goods. They did not care about the ongoing, large-scale disappearance of jobs in traditional Soviet-era industries, or about massive delays in paying wages to Russian employees, or about miserly pensions, or about the looming threat to social service agencies. They got the opportunity to consume various goods, in quantities only dreamed of in Soviet times, and thus they were willing to absolve the ruling group of its responsibility even for the drastic worsening of the quality of law enforcement and the resulting threats to individual safety, as well as for the lack of high-quality civic and economic institutions and of a functioning competition-based political system. They were ready to disregard all of this in exchange for the opportunity to raise their consumption and social status through their own efforts and some good luck (such as the fact that they happened to be in the right place at the right time).

It was natural for the political elite at the time to seek—and, by and large, to find—the coveted social base of support among these people. It was precisely this stratum, whose members identified themselves as entrepreneurs and as the new economic elite, that helped the ruling group, in the mid-1990s, to secure at least a degree of legitimation of its power through the elections of 1996. This same stratum also helped the ruling group to overcome the shocks of hyperinflation and of the taming of it through ruthless slashing of social expenditures and public investment. It helped the ruling group survive Russia's debt default and the banking crisis of 1998, the psychological shock of Russia's de facto defeat in the war against secessionists in the Caucasus, and the loss of Russia's superpower status in international relations.

It was also natural that neither public employees and other strata that were economically dependent on the government nor those many Soviet industrial and agricultural workers who had turned into a newly marginalized class could provide an alternative social base of government support at the time. As for the top brass of uniformed agencies, the ruling group could win their deference by giving them an opportunity to experience all the benefits of wielding the real power of coercion on their own, free from intrusive monitoring by the Communist Party bosses and security services, which had constrained their freedom of action in Soviet times.

Thus, during that relatively brief period of a transitional—or, so to speak, an immature—authoritarianism, the characteristics of the ruling group's social base of support were largely skewed toward the model of authoritarian modernization. Under this model, as we know, the leading role is played by capital owners and the "aristocracy" of uniformed services, while the working masses are reduced to beasts of burden, toiling under Spartan conditions compared to those of a modern welfare state, with a minimal government-sponsored safety net. The civilian bureaucracy, overall, was already in an undoubtedly privileged position. Yet, at the time, only the tiny upper crust of this stratum, virtually an exclusive club among them, could claim to be the dominant, ruling force in the country. The bulk of this bureaucracy did not feel that they were the core, the social base, or even the beneficiaries of the political system that was taking shape at the time and has reached its maturity today.

Nonetheless, as the system was ripening, these social strata began to perceive themselves differently, and the ruling circle changed its approach toward them. The elites increasingly came to realize that, in spite of Russia's rising incomes, the country was not getting any closer to the West, the most developed core of world capitalism, and was, at best, sliding along in a circular orbit, making rounds without any visible hope of joining the global club of the mighty and the powerful. With this understanding, members of the ruling circle also experienced a change in their thinking about the kind of society in which they were going to live in the coming decades. And it became obvious to them that only natural resources—mainly oil and gas, and more precisely their export abroad—generate the large financial flows that the ruling group is capable of detecting, tracking, and utilizing; therefore, there was less and less need to seek the support of the entrepreneurial class.

Russia's elite believe that such natural resources belong to the state and not to the companies that extract or export them, even if these companies are privately owned. And because the ruling group genuinely views itself as equivalent to the state itself, it does not see any need to seek the goodwill or assistance of private business owners in order to control the revenues generated by the exploitation of these resources. Rather, the opposite is true: the government decides who among the entrepreneurs will get a chance to have a piece of the pie or get a contract to service this national feeding trough of natural resource utilization, and how much each one will get. Moreover, from the point of view of the authorities, giving private businesses a formal role in making money off natural resources achieves nothing except to nurture their illusions about actually owning those resources; it also feeds their aspirations to control related resources and financial flows on their own, which means claiming a significant role in the governance of state and society.

The ruling group could not conceivably let this happen. It was only logical for them to take over—not just in de facto but also in legal terms—the key sources of oil and gas revenues and to place them under the control of the government as their "natural" owner. Hence the setting up of new, giant, government-owned companies—Rosneft and Gazprom Neft—to work in oil extraction; hence the de facto nationalization of oil and gas companies Sibneft and Yukos; and hence Gazprom's official monopolistic hold on the export of natural gas. Most important of all, the authorities must show private "capitalists" that all resources in the country, and all large-scale financial assets based on these resources, are—by default and because this is "the way it is"—the property of the highest government authority, to be used by others only for a period of time and only with the permission of the Kremlin. The property rights on these assets belong to the state (that is, to the ruling circle), are inalienable in principle, and cannot be entrusted to the "elemental" forces of the market.

For private business outside of the resources industry (which, of course, in today's Russia means primarily trade, finance, and business services), in the context of the economic system that has taken shape in the country, the further a business is removed from government monitoring and control, the higher the profitability and the safety of the business will be. Therefore, it would be risky or even naive on the part of the authorities to look within this stratum for a subgroup that would constitute a potential social base for them or, in broader terms, for any institution whatsoever.

On the other hand, the increasing ability of the government to amass control over financial resources, primarily those generated by rent extraction in the oil and gas industry, has enabled the authorities to develop a different social base for themselves, consisting of groups that are dependent upon government payments. In the first decade of the century, such groups' level of consumption grew rapidly, due to the steady growth of these government expenditures. This large stratum includes employees of government agencies and their families; those whose well-being depends upon government contracts, not just on the federal but also on the regional and municipal levels; and recipients of pensions, social assistance, and other public payments.

It was from among these groups that the Kremlin drew support for itself in the elections, and partly in the process of governing during the first decade of the twenty-first century. These groups were the prime targets of propaganda efforts that were plain to see in the broadcasting policies of the national TV channels. During this period, these TV companies significantly shifted their emphases and preferences with regard to the political tenor of their broadcasting. Previously, in the 1990s, their primary message had consisted of urging energetic and ambitious individuals to get away from dependence upon the government and to transform themselves into independent players in the capitalist game, even if that meant failing to scrupulously abide by the laws. Now, in the aughts, these very same media increasingly exhibited the tendency to engage with the aforementioned groups that were dependent on government payments, to cater to their priorities and their distinctive ways of thinking. Among the propaganda spins that fit into this trend were the glorification of stability and the ominous daily reminders about the "wild 1990s" as Russia's dark age; the relatively frequent pay raises for government employees and contractors;[12]

and, finally, an almost officially nurtured nostalgia for Soviet times, which celebrated the era's "heroes of labor" and "intelligentsia of simple backgrounds" and cultivated the notion of a modest but growing well-being.

After the turn of the century, the social status of the government bureaucracy undoubtedly started to increase, and its actual material and intangible resources were growing conspicuously. Never mind that the portrayal of this class in the mass-oriented propaganda was still primarily negative or that the ruling circle was putting upon these bureaucrats the onus of responsibility for the many outrageous things in everyday life and beyond that caused irritation among the masses of Russians. Initially, the bureaucracy's rising fortunes were mostly caused by the authorities' informal permission for it to get more assertive in its behavior.

By the end of that decade, however, the official compensation for members of the government bureaucracy, starting with its upper crust, also began to grow exponentially, while the gap between them and the majority of employees in Russia became unprecedentedly large. This in itself was an indicator of the changing role of this class within the framework of Russia's authoritarianism. Unsurprisingly, virtually every survey of professional and career preferences among young Russians, beginning from 2005–2010, showed that government service was becoming an increasingly popular choice, while young people's interest in entrepreneurial career opportunities was declining.

On top of that, the aughts were also characterized by the development and strengthening of pervasive corporatism in Russia's political system, which makes authoritarian rule significantly more potent, more rigid, and irreversible in terms of demodernizing the country. This corporatism is represented by the Eurasianist-style vertical hierarchy of power, ideologically inherited from the Stalinist model. Within this framework, the supreme government authority is perceived as the "director" of the entire country, in charge of everything, with all others being his employees "in the line of duty," and every entity, all the way to one's home or office desk, is a department or a subdivision of his megacorporation.

In this setting, which is rather unusual even for authoritarian regimes, society as a factor in political life gets completely erased from the map. Quite frequently, sociologists are noticing seemingly paradoxical responses of the mass consciousness to certain stimuli, sometimes in trivial, everyday situations, and these responses suggest, first and foremost, that public consciousness has morphed into the mentality of corporate servants who are fearful of the possibility of getting "fired" by their boss and thus of losing everything that remains of their well-being. Thus, in this regard, too, we are witnessing the consolidation of a political system in Russia that is quite accurately described as peripheral authoritarianism.

THE WEAKNESS OF INSTITUTIONS

Finally, analysts and observers have not paid due attention to the weakness of institutions, which is yet another feature of Russia's peripheral authoritarianism. Strictly speaking, the issue of whether institutions are weak or strong does not have any fixed relationship to the choice of a political system, such as the choice between an authoritarian and a competition-based system, though it is quite possible that there is some correlation between the two. Overall, under any political system, whether an autocracy or genuine multiparty parliamentary rule, weakness in a society's institutions diminishes the capacity of those institutions to manage societal developments. The opposite is also true: in instances where any of these political systems serve well, or relatively well, the interests of national development, they provide for the establishment of robust institutions that will ensure the continuity of the policies of the dominant class and their independence from the personal whims and prejudices of individual members of the ruling circle.

Certainly, authoritarian systems generally tend to produce regimes that are centered upon the personality of an unchallenged leader standing atop the ruling circle, embodying the regime, and playing the most important role in the process of making key decisions. Nevertheless, such a leader cannot and, in practice, never does substitute for the complex machinery of a modern state, let alone supplant the functioning of multiple institutions, without which it is impossible to conduct any sophisticated, productive economic activities, develop a modern social and business infrastructure, or even maintain basic order in any relatively advanced society. From this point of view, the task of constructing workable and efficient institutions is relevant for any government that has a sense of responsibility for its actions—and this includes leader-oriented dictatorships, as long as at least one of their goals is to secure steady development for their society and country.

Moreover, only the establishment of viable institutions can ensure an unperturbed succession, without catastrophes and upheavals, at the point when, for whatever reason, the individual resource of the man at the top has been used up. Leader-oriented regimes are bound to expire, at least for biological reasons, if nothing else, and in the absence of such institutions, it is highly likely that the end of these regimes will create a void at the top of the power hierarchy, followed by a no-holds-barred fight for control of the levers of power, a drastic increase in uncertainty, and deterioration of the business environment. Under the worst scenario, it may lead to chaos and a breakdown in state governance for a very extensive period of time.

It is plain to see that autocracies of a modernizing type, even markedly leader-oriented, personality-driven regimes (such as existed, for example, in South Korea), have managed to create and develop the social, political, and economic institutions that were generally capable of meeting the challenges of their time. These institutions were able to secure the basic continuity of policies during times of leadership succession at the top and to provide for the increasing complexity and modernization of their economy and society. Essentially, this and only this can serve as the precondition for a transition, over the long haul, from an authoritarian to a competition-based type of political system featuring alternation of ruling groups in power, elections as the tool to adjudicate the outcomes of competition among the teams contending for power, and, at the same time, strict, collectively set limitations on the range of potential activities in which the competing teams and the political forces behind these teams may engage.

Meanwhile, an authoritarian regime of a peripheral type—the kind that tends to produce stagnation and dependence upon the core of the world economy—is characterized by its typical inability to build viable, let alone successfully functioning, institutions. Not only is it bound to inevitably descend into one-man rule centered upon the cult of the leader, but also it has to switch the mode of governance to "manual," practicing micro-management from the top. That is, the institutional mechanisms and processes that automatically regulate economic, social, and political developments according to preestablished scripts either do not function without continuous intervention from the higher-ups or keep changing their modes of operation according to signals received from the supreme ruler, who has a virtually unlimited freedom of managerial decision-making.

Furthermore, such a regime of "manual" governance from the top traps the system in a situation where, once micromanagement is applied, it becomes impossible to go back to normal government functioning. From this point, continuous intervention is required just to keep government operating on a regular basis, since any deviations from standard operations are no longer automatically adjusted by the institutions operating on their own. Instead, fixing these deviations now requires special decisions to be made, as a rule, with the participation of the autocrat himself. As a result, the system becomes increasingly more dependent upon the accuracy and the effectiveness of decisions made at the top of the pyramid. At the same time, the likelihood of flawed or suboptimal decisions by the autocrat naturally increases, if only because of the inevitable exhaustion of his physical, psychological, and intellectual resources.

This is essentially what has been happening in Russia throughout the post-Soviet period. From the beginning, the process of developing legislative institutions took an extremely regrettable turn. The unsuccessful experience of the first post-Soviet legislative bodies—the Congress of People's Deputies and its Supreme Council—could still be explained by the disconnect between the institutions formed during the Soviet period and their changed environment. However, the new legislative body that was established on the basis of the new constitution of 1993—Russia's Federal Assembly—was subjected to constant negativity from the media and the government. The only plausible explanation for this negativity was the inability of the Kremlin—whose character and structure, already in the 1990s, was undoubtedly authoritarian—to develop working relations with this institution, which did not fit into the developing framework of authoritarian governance.

In the first decade of the twenty-first century, this issue was resolved in the manner that the ruling circle believed would be the simplest. They suppressed all kinds of dissent and took away opportunities for influencing legislation, ramming through the Duma all the decisions that were made by the actual powers that be ensconced in the Kremlin, without any debate or any compromises. To achieve this, the Kremlin formed a monolithic pro-government majority of legislators, controlled from the outside and based on rigid discipline and the unquestioning execution of the Kremlin's decisions.

However, such a simple and seemingly efficient solution to the problem of having a parliamentary institution that was superfluous in an autocracy came with a certain price. By effectively stripping the legislature of any real influence in political decision-making, the ruling circle also deprived it of prestige and legitimacy among Russia's political class and general population. In the short term, this would seem to be convenient for the Kremlin, since it accentuates the absence of alternatives to its rule, which is so important for any authoritarian power. In the long run, however, it makes both the political system and the state itself more vulnerable and fragile. Now every complication and every crisis carries the risk of a potential loss of control over the situation, and this may even be more likely, given the lack of institutions endowed with legitimacy and able to compensate for the breakdown of state governance resulting from erroneous actions or inaction of the authorities.[13]

Such a situation is especially risky for Russia, which has neither a functioning and legitimate representative body nor any alternative supreme authority that could hold power if its current organization breaks down. In addition, it is precisely the inability of Russia's present-day parliament to exert any real influence that strips it of its legitimacy in the eyes of various societal groups and government agencies. As we know, today's Russia has neither a hereditary monarch nor a religious body with any real authority sanctified by tradition, nor does the military serve as an autonomous political institution. Thus, there is a high risk of a major breakdown of state governance, with unpredictable consequences for the country.

But the weakness of the Federal Assembly as the representative body is certainly not the only issue. All the other institutions that are essential for a modern state exhibit extreme weakness and an incapacity to perform as they should. This is one of the manifestations of the peripheral character of Russia's authoritarianism.

The challenges faced by the judiciary during the first decade of the century, for example, were discussed frequently and in much detail by many observers, and there were attempts to reform it, yet none of this has had any significant impact in terms of making the judiciary perform more effectively than before. Perhaps the best evidence of the failure of Russia's judiciary is that those in control of Russian financial assets, including government assets, continue to incorporate their firms in foreign countries and offshore tax havens, on a mass scale. The owners of these entities justify their actions mainly by citing the "convenience" of the administrative and court procedures involved in managing these assets outside of the purview of Russia's judiciary (in addition to the implicitly acknowledged political risks of operating in Russia). It is almost universally admitted that Russian courts are very hard to use in defending one's title to a property.

In today's Russia, it is just as questionable whether one can count upon the judiciary as an institution to protect individuals against wrongful persecution by law enforcement or other government agencies. At the very least, there has been too much evidence that the judiciary has become infected along with everyone else and that it displays a dismissive attitude toward the law that is typical of peripheral-type authoritarian regimes. In making their decisions, judges are practically able to ignore existing laws and regulations without risking any negative consequences for themselves.

Meanwhile, other significant institutions—those involved in law enforcement as well as those of a purely civilian nature—are relatively weak as well. And the main issue here is not merely the discrepancy between the scope of their mandated functions and the means and resources at these agencies' disposal, or in their overlapping functions and areas of responsibility, or in the conflicts of interest, all of which are among the traditional challenges facing bureaucracy. There is a problem of a more fundamental nature, as I will discuss.

If we dispense with the facade and the superficial rhetoric, institutions are ultimately the norms and rules that are observed. They rely upon a tradition, or at least upon an acknowledgement of the need for it, and do not get altered on a whim to suit the needs of individual power holders at any particular moment. The distinctive feature of a peripheral authoritarianism is its denial of any steady long-term rules of operation that form the gist and the basis of public institutions in a developed society. Within the framework of such a system, institutions are no more than bureaucratic agencies set up to resolve specific tasks, the parameters of which are defined by the supreme authority. Hence, they play no autonomous role in shaping the direction of the subsequent development of the system.

Likewise, the guiding principles and considerations that these agencies use to accomplish the tasks assigned to them may easily and frequently change, depending on the needs of the moment and even the personal preferences of those who, at any given time, exert the most influence upon the views of the boss at the top of the one-man autocracy. As a result, the rules within the system end up being fluid, unsteady, and incapable of functioning as a glue to hold society together.

Essentially, this is precisely what we observed at the beginning of the twenty-first century in Russia. The hopes that economic stability would bring with it stable norms of everyday life embodied in robust institutions have not materialized. Today, just as at the turn of the century, Russia still has an unstable legal system, a system of law enforcement that acts selectively and is largely not functioning, and a continuously fluctuating set of rules on taxation, on retirement systems, on social, demographic, educational, and migration policies, and the like. This is precisely why the school system, local governments, territorial and cultural communities, political parties, and the entrenched mass media have failed to engage in the task of stabilizing relations in society. (The media must be the subject of a separate discussion, but it is important for our present purposes that their mainstream part has been unable to assume the role of a stabilizing, consolidating institution that would shape the boundaries of public consensus and tame the incursions of the political fringe across these boundaries.)

Finally, it must be noted that this institutional weakness has become a major constraint and a brake upon the development of the sophisticated financial and economic institutions characteristic of developed economies. Thus, over the past decade, the process of forming the institutional infrastructure of modern finance, which started in Russia in the 1990s, has ground to a halt. This is due to the deficiencies of all the institutions mentioned here, first and foremost the judiciary, as well as of the system of government–business relations in the areas of legislation and law enforcement that goes together with the development of finance.

Therefore, in the institutional sphere as well, Russia's authoritarianism displays the characteristics of a peripheral type. Its stagnation-prone qualities and social and economic ineffectiveness in accomplishing the tasks of development are related not to authoritarianism as such but rather to its specific positioning within the system of global capitalism. This positioning makes it possible for Russia to exist as a second-tier, dependent element of this system and, hence, lowers the requirements that it has to meet in global economic development. That is, within this configuration, the weakness of institutions is both a cause and a consequence of Russian capitalism's peripheral role, and this is at least one reason why all of the authorities' rhetoric about modernization and about upgrading to the level of world economic leaders remains but empty talk, disjointed pieces of wishful thinking that, quite predictably, are never followed by any practical action.

4

THE FUTURE OF AUTOCRACY IN RUSSIA

What Do We Have to Tolerate (and for How Long)?

In the previous chapters, I have analyzed the political system that has taken shape in Russia and have identified its essential features as a political organization within peripheral capitalism that allows us to characterize it as a peripheral authoritarianism. This means that the political system that has taken shape in Russia is a leader-oriented authoritarianism, with all its typical traits, including monopolistic control of one ruling circle or team, single-handedly led by one person, over all government institutions in the country; the absence of working mechanisms to ensure an involuntary replacement of the ruling circle with another group of people; and the ideology of a unified and indivisible power as the universal principle of governance. It also views the law as an auxiliary tool to use in ruling society, but it does not limit this power or make it accountable.

The economic underpinning of this power has been the ability to allocate administrative rent, derived from monopolistic control over major economic assets. This enables the ruling circle and its leader to command the political life of society as they see fit, by using their control over most of the financial flows and information/propaganda resources—even if, formally, they preserve the channels for feedback from society and the mechanisms of political competition (including a multiparty system and periodic national and local elections).

Thus, the extent of the authorities' power and the limits of what they can do within the existing framework are primarily determined by the amount of administrative rent they are able to extract and to distribute. The larger the amount, the more opportunities there are for the ruling group to maintain its control over society without applying direct physical pressure. The system's ability to neutralize potentially destabilizing external impacts also plays an important role. The ruling circle must possess the requisite tools and resources to give them an edge over outside forces that are capable of influencing key segments of society in a direction that is undesirable for the system.

All of this constitutes the common, generic features of authoritarian rule as such. In today's Russia, these are combined with significant characteristics and elements resulting from the peripheral character of Russia's capitalism. This is evident in the underdeveloped and undiversified economy; the absence of an economic and political elite embedded in society and its history; the extreme weakness of public institutions, such as political parties, with support in various strata of society; the failure of representative bodies to serve as platforms for interaction among political forces in the pursuit of mutually acceptable solutions; a lack of executive agencies with clearly defined purposes and responsibilities; the failure of the law as the regulator of relations within society; and so on.

Ultimately, this is a manifestation of the dependence of Russian capitalism upon global centers. This dependence accounts, on the one hand, for the lack of autonomy of Russia's business elites within Russia and their subsequent migration outside of Russia's territory and, on the other hand, for their anti-Western sentiment, which is generated by their sense of their own parochialism, their subordinate position, and their vulnerability.

All of these features, taken together, help to explain the characteristic traits of Russia's authoritarianism. There is the authorities' lack of a sense of their public service mission. There is a reliance upon corruption as a method and instrument of governance, the general public's lack of faith in the possibility of change ("There is no other way, no matter what we do"), and xenophobia as the basis of political stability. There is a pursuit of isolation from any external influences. Finally, there is a cult of peculiar "traditional values," used to justify the existence of deep gulfs of socioeconomic inequality and the population's generally low levels of personal and public consumption relative to the consumption in global centers like the United States and Europe.

At the same time, none of this is exclusive to the global periphery. Moreover, corruption and purposeful conditioning of public opinion by the establishment exist in the global centers in much more intricate forms, and thus on a much larger scale, than on the periphery. The difference is that, in the peripheral-type economies and societies, these are used less for the redistribution of the products of development and more as a universal instrument of governance. Furthermore, reliance upon these instruments largely makes development itself impossible, as it precludes the use of more sophisticated and more efficient tools of governance.

As has been shown, Russia developed this kind of political system gradually, step by step, but quite consistently and steadily, and its shape was to some degree objectively conditioned. The outcome of this was the formation of the full-blown autocracy with markedly peripheral traits and tendency toward stagnation that we see in Russia today. In my opinion, this is best illustrated by the events of 2014, when all of these attributes became fully formed and plain to see. By an arbitrary decision of the president, who was given the legal authority to use military force abroad with no reservation or prior discussion by the parliament's upper house, Crimea was taken under control and driven toward annexation, and the separatist movement in southeast Ukraine was initiated and supported. To justify these steps, a new edition of the "Eurasian" empire-building ideological campaign was launched, presented as an alternative to European values. The propaganda machine also resorted to lies to deny responsibility for the downing of a Malaysian Airline Boeing 777, which resulted in heavy civilian casualties.

However, it seems not enough to simply record as a given the fact of the formation of such a political system in post-Soviet Russia. If we claim to understand the logic of this system's development and functioning, then we must to some extent envision the possibilities of its evolution and the scenarios for its future. Despite the infinite possibilities of tomorrow, and knowing that future scenarios always include uncertainty, we still can outline some patterns of development inherent in socioeconomic systems. These patterns are familiar to us from world history and are accounted for by the logic of relationships among social phenomena and events. We shall now investigate how these patterns are playing out in Russia.

THE FUTURE OF THE SYSTEM: IS IT PREDICTABLE?

The first question that I would like to tackle is whether the evolution of a political system may be predetermined in any way at all. Are there any templates that history uses to chart a system's trajectory?

In my past writings, I have noted that the developments at the turn of the century prompted many of us to reassess our views on this subject. Only twenty years ago, mainstream thinkers and experts in the West tended to believe that, sooner or later (more precisely, in the coming decades), all societies were going to end up accepting the basic principles of political order that are most often called "liberal democracy." These principles include the separation of power among government's distinctive branches, the legal impossibility of usurping power and establishing a monopoly on its exercise, competition among political parties for the right to form the executive branch of government, elections to representative bodies based upon universal and equal voting rights, the supremacy of law and respect for minority rights, and a number of other, second-level principles. Essentially, these principles are inherent (or at least are supposed to be inherent) in the competition-based model of the political organization of the state. These principles not only were recognized as universal basic values but also were viewed (in the spirit of Francis Fukuyama's "end of history") as the inevitable outcome of a progressive development of any existing national community, regardless of the historical and cultural differences among them. From this point of view, any autocratic regimes still existing at the end of the twentieth century were viewed as anachronistic holdovers that the course of history itself was going to remove from the stage in a relatively short period of time.

Even today, this point of view is at the very least prevalent among Western academics and experts, though not nearly to the extent that it was fifteen or twenty years ago. Under the influence of several factors, the model of a "universal future" began to recede from its dominant position and was partly modified, with its ongoing reassessment going in at least two directions. On the one hand, the theory of multiple civilizations has abruptly gained popularity. This theory views many of the tensions in international (as well as in interethnic and interfaith) relations as an irreconcilable and intractable "clash of civilizations." Strictly speaking, this theory was virtually ubiquitous during the Middle Ages, though it was described in the simple and relatively unsophisticated forms that suited those times, and, with some qualifications, it was part of the state ideology of most countries—to the extent that we can apply the term "ideology" to that era in history. In the second half of the twentieth century, it seemed that faith in the power of a humanistic approach to the world and in the significance of progress and universal "democratic values," as well as the spread of the notions of political correctness during the century's final few decades, had completely marginalized the theory of the "clash of civilizations" and that it was disappearing from the stage. Meanwhile, the values that were usually called "European" had seemingly achieved the status of "universal human values."

Nevertheless, by the end of the twentieth century the theory of the multiplicity of civilizations suddenly started acquiring new followers, including followers in the Western world, and, so to speak, becoming legitimized in the scholarly community.[1] Furthermore, the basic tenets of this theory began to shape the practical activities of politicians in such areas as foreign and defense policy and even, at least to some extent, in the humanitarian sphere. For example, the practice of using double standards, which is widespread in today's international relations, is essentially nothing but a practical political reflection of the concept of "different human civilizations." In this framework, the actions of one's own civilization that its representatives view as acceptable and ethical appear unacceptable and unethical when practiced by others. And the opposite is also true: what is viewed as completely unacceptable, an "absolute evil" in civic terms, within one's own political system is recognized as not only acceptable but even convenient and useful within political systems organized in somewhat different ways. This framework can serve as a convenient tool for dominant groups seeking to consolidate their power, as it is easier to rally mass support for themselves by identifying an alternative "civilization" as a common enemy.

At the same time, the assumptions about a "natural" universal world order, which had been characteristic of mainstream Western thought at the end of the twentieth century, were being subjected to reassessment from yet another end. Namely, it became increasingly in vogue to view international relations as nothing more but a geopolitical game. In this perspective, strong players wrestle with each other to expand their respective spheres of influence, while the weaker ones try to gain as much advantage for themselves as they can, using the opportunities provided by this struggle and its associated tensions. From this point of view, even the disappearance or a significant relaxation of global ideological conflicts (as, for example, the de facto disappearance from the international stage of so-called world communism as a global ideological alternative to "liberal democracy") does not alter the logic of world politics as the struggle among various states over influence, power, and resources.

To put it otherwise, this current of thought denies the primacy of ideology in international relations, viewing it as merely one of the factors that shape the configuration of the struggle among competing global players. Accordingly, in this framework, the blurring of ideological differences is bound to be compensated for by other factors that justify the need to play the global game and win control over resources (broadly defined, including the resource of political power). Meanwhile, the essence of global politics as a game remains the same, from time immemorial to our own day. Zbigniew Brzezinski, the author of *The Grand Chessboard*, is often cited as virtually the foremost representative of this analytical current.

In reality, this logic is indeed pronounced, though not as much in present-day writings on geopolitics as in the ongoing commentary by practicing politicians, intended to shape the opinions and decisions of others. Yet this way of thinking does not and never has had anything novel or groundbreaking in it. Often it is essentially nothing more than an extrapolation into our times of the perennial view of international relations as a tussle among princes and states pursuing expansion of their own power. It is nothing but an attempt to thwart the temporary dominance of "politically correct" views about the practical feasibility of establishing a minimally harmonious and sustainable universal world order in the future.

In any case, the universal convergence of various political systems on the basis of universal liberal democratic values, which so recently seemed to be forthcoming and unavoidable, is already viewed by many as a utopian vision. Although authoritarian political systems are still viewed as most likely to collapse or to be transformed into competition-based systems, in the intermediate future this probability no longer looks as obvious and inevitable as it once did. At present, the trajectory and time frame of the evolution of existing autocracies are seen by developed countries as more convoluted than they appeared just recently.

It is increasingly acknowledged that the expectations of the impending, ineluctable collapse of all dictatorships and "tyrannies" as a result of the spread of education and political activism among the masses have been mistaken and impractical. There is also a growing recognition that the process of liberal democracy conquering the world is a lengthy one and, on some terrains, is easily reversible. Granted, the vision of a competition-based ("democratic") political system, with broad guarantees of individual rights and the rights of various minorities, as the decisive stage of the political history of the world is still prevalent in the public consciousness. Yet, at present, this vision accepts, at the very least, the possibility of a protracted existence and internal development of alternative political systems.

These alternative systems include various types of autocracies, including theocracies and semifeudal systems of rule based on direct personal service of local power holders to more powerful authorities and on outright violence by warlords or field commanders. They also include totalitarian regimes built upon the theories of ethnic or ideological superiority, as well as all kinds of mixed and transitional systems. It is worth noting that the time horizon of their existence is no longer estimated to be just a few, or ten, or fifteen years at best; instead, it is expected that they may be able to exist and go through changes over extended periods of time while possibly enjoying high degrees of stability.

I believe that this relatively new approach to the potential prospects of existing autocracies is much closer to reality than the prior notion of their predetermined internal exhaustion, their lack of capacity to adapt to existing realities and their looming collapse. Moreover, the direction of changes within these systems is not an a priori given; it may vary greatly depending on circumstances. In some instances, these changes may result in the consolidation and even improved effectiveness of the monopolistic exercise of power by the ruling group. Of course, as the society under their rule and the tasks they face become more complex, the advantages of a competition-based political system over its authoritarian counterpart become increasingly more tangible—both from the point of view of efficient resource utilization and in terms of lowering the risks of major blunders and ultimately of a potential collapse of statehood as such.

Nonetheless, it must be noted that several factors present in the world today increase the possibility of a protracted survival of authoritarian political systems, even though these systems are out of sync with their surroundings. The first of these factors is the long-term division of the world into the "center" and the "periphery," with the periphery facing objectively lower demands than does the center in terms of the efficiency of governance and of its success in accomplishing its socioeconomic tasks. To put it simply, to serve as a supplier of certain kinds of raw materials to the developed world, a peripheral country is by no means required to build a modern, socially responsible system of governance that would ensure progress in science and technology or to strike a balance among various social, territorial, and ethnocultural groups, let alone to undertake an effective pursuit of economic, technological, or political leadership in the world. To serve as a raw materials provider, it is quite sufficient to have the minimally required material infrastructure and to protect it against destructive forces, which is a manageable task for even the most archaic authoritarian systems. Dozens of countries have managed to fit into the world economy in one way or another, even if only as a remote and isolated outskirt, without having a functionally proficient modern state or even planning to develop one in the foreseeable future.

Another factor consists of the objective changes in the economic underpinnings of contemporary developed societies, which have been reducing the significance of control over territories as a source of the country's well-being. Merely two hundred years ago, a decline in the power and effectiveness of a given state would almost inevitably bring with it the loss of control over territories, to the advantage of its more powerful neighbors, leading to a change in the composition of the ruling circle, if not of the entire system. Today, in contrast, weak and ineffective states may exist for a long time without being viewed by stronger powers as a potentially desirable acquisition that they would like to incorporate or to control. The prosperity of the developed world is increasingly based on sources that have nothing to do with controlling territories of others. In my previous book, *Realeconomik*, I wrote quite a bit about rent derived from one's historical advantage (historical rent) and rent on intellectual capital (innovation rent), which serve as the sources of large-scale revenues for developed countries without their having to maintain control over foreign territories.[2] It is easy for developed countries to gain access, through international trade and investment, to raw mineral or energy resources that are physically located in specific territories. Under these circumstances, even the so-called "failed states" can linger for decades without being physically taken over by anyone willing to take advantage of their infirmity.

Finally, the third factor that would seem to increase the possibility of the protracted survival of authoritarian political systems is a general softening of the developed part of the world, sometimes called its weakness, its spinelessness, the extinction of its spirit, and so on. This is a condition of society in which everyday life and the relative well-being of most of one's fellow citizens (who are also voters and whose sentiments have to be taken into account in politics) are becoming more valuable than the vision of a global transformation, of bringing other parts of the world in line with one's own views about the desirable organization of society, and other similar collective and supranational goals. This helps to explain why countries that view themselves as the political leaders of the Western world, with a mission to "spread democracy" everywhere, are actually unwilling to expend any substantial amount of financial or other resources toward this purpose. These countries widely tout their support for the "struggle for freedom," and yet, even with regard to autocracies whose prospects for an institutional transformation seem to be quite realistic, their support is typically limited to rhetorical stunts, along with very modest financial contributions to those whom they identify as the opposition to authoritarian rule and as "friends of the West." And when some of these Western countries resort to costly military campaigns to advance these goals, as the United States did in the Iraq campaign, for instance, they typically do it in response to specific situations and to domestic political needs, which does not have much to do with any strategy of promoting democracy. Moreover, the new regimes to emerge after such campaigns are rarely a significant improvement over their predecessors.

Therefore, if present-day authoritarian regimes ever lose their grip on society, it usually is caused not by some external impact or by a lack of international competitiveness; rather, it typically comes about for internal reasons. Foremost among these internal causes is the regime's inability to ensure that the economic, political, and social developments within its jurisdiction remain controllable. And this failure, in turn, may occur simply because several things go wrong at the same time or, more often, because mistakes or erratic decisions are made by the ruling circle or the autocratic leader. Absent the mechanisms for the system to autocorrect these errors, the regime is led into a dead end, where it is incapable of meeting the challenges it faces.

Nevertheless, there are certain patterns in the evolution of political systems, and this must also be applicable to the peripheral authoritarian system that has taken shape in today's post-Soviet Russia. Despite all the caveats and uncertainties mentioned earlier, some of the changes within the system are more probable than others, and the direction of these changes is determined both by the system's internal logic and by its environment. Since both of these variables are fairly predictable, we can also forecast and describe the most probable scenarios for prospective developments in Russia.

PUTIN'S THIRD TERM AND HIS NEW SET OF POLICIES

Identifying and describing the highest-probability scenarios for the future has been made simpler by the fact that, starting in 2014, Putin's authoritarian tendencies, which had been dormant or barely nascent over the previous ten to fifteen years, have now come to the fore. Earlier, it was not clear how fast they might develop and how far they might go. Even now, there is still no full clarity in this regard, but at least Putin's authoritarian impulse has emerged in a much more discernible way, and the probability that the current direction of developments will be reversed is many times lower than it used to be.

What I mean is mainly the sum total of the facts that have become clear to Russians since 2012, once the so-called castling of 2008 (whereby Vladimir Putin and Dmitry Medvedev switched their official positions, with Putin becoming prime minister and Medvedev president) was reversed and Putin began his third presidential term as the undisputed head of Russia's ruling circle. This may be labeled Putin's new agenda, but in reality there is nothing fundamentally new about it; it is just an acceleration and a continuous unshackling of the trends that were already inherent in the political system and the public consciousness.

Russia's ruling circle has intensified its ideological and political confrontation with the center of the global capitalism, and, as players in world politics, they have conspicuously refused to abide by the rules proposed by the center. These elites have been striving to develop their own official ideology and to actually make it the government ideology, that is, to impose and defend it with all the might of government resources and power. They have tended not just to put a squeeze upon any organized alternative political current but also to restrict as much as possible all kinds of opposition, including intellectual opposition, which has no real resources that would enable it to pose any noticeable threat to the authorities.

It is easily noted that all these trends are closely intertwined, so that each of them makes perfect sense in light of the others, while also reinforcing them. The outcome is a quite powerful trend pushing the system as a whole toward totalitarianism, even if it is not as in-your-face as the most familiar twentieth-century political systems of this kind. In any case, the model of the political organization of society toward which Russia has been clearly drifting in the past several years contains several features of totalitarian systems. These features include the dominance of one set of views in the public sphere, affirmed and protected by the government, and the portrayal of any alternative views as inimical to the state and the people. The government also has a tendency toward the deliberate isolation of society from all external influences, which are interpreted as being directed against the nation, hostile, and debilitating for society and the country, as they induce Russians to commit treason. I also observe the brainwashing of the public to believe in these mythical threats even as they also face real ones. In sum, the people at the top of the power system are increasingly portrayed to the Russian people as the supreme authority, whose decisions can no longer be questioned.

THE OUTSIDE WORLD AS THE ENEMY

The first element of Putin's new set of policies, noted earlier, is its orientation toward an outwardly uncompromising rejection of the rules of international politics that are set by the powers of the global capitalist "core"—the United States and the large European powers that determine the policies of the European Union. Plainly, this attitude is nothing completely new, nor is it unexpected. The critique of the rules of the game established by the West has been an important component of post-Soviet Russia's domestic and foreign policy for at least the past fifteen years. Suffice it to recall such incidents from the recent history of international relations as the crisis in the former Yugoslavia, and the EU and NATO interference in that crisis; the war of the NATO members against the regime of Saddam Hussein and the subsequent occupation of Iraq; the tense arguments between Russia and the United States over the deployment of American antimissile defense systems; the enlargement of NATO through its incorporation of Eastern Europe; the Russian–Georgian conflict of 2008, resulting in large-scale military operations; and so on.

Each of these events led to acute disagreements between Russia and leading Western powers. These disagreements not only narrowed the opportunity for potential constructive interaction between the two sides but also were actively exploited by all parties in the process of shaping their domestic public opinion. Every time these disagreements sharpened, both sides became increasingly convinced that there was not and could not be a consensus about the rules of behavior in situations of conflict, and thus that any diplomatic efforts to reduce the differences, or at least to find some common ground on issues, could only have a limited and temporary effect.

Meanwhile, the Western powers predictably assumed, as something self-evident, that their role as the core of world capitalism (and thus of the contemporary world as a whole) entitled them to use their advantage to set the rules of international behavior according to their own perceptions of justice and international law. Thus, they viewed anybody else's attempts to resist playing by the rules established in this manner as negative behavior, and they considered the initiators of these attempts to be, at best, spoilers of the West's political triumph and, at worst, enemies trying to subvert the established world order. Even before recent allegations of Russian interference in European and American elections, Western countries had settled upon a view of Russia as intent upon spoiling their party. For their part, Russia's leadership and the public opinion that it controls had convinced themselves that playing by the West's rules is of no benefit for Russia but in fact works to Russia's detriment, leading to losses every single time.

Yet, starting in about 2013 or 2014, the disagreements between Russia and the West became increasingly acute. With every turn of events around Libya and Syria, and then with the intense political crisis in Ukraine,[3] the Kremlin became convinced that Russia's subordination to the rules that were being set by the West could only lead to Western disregard of the Kremlin's opinion and interests, as understood by its denizens. When the Kremlin takes what the West considers a "constructive" stance, Russia does not and cannot derive any benefit from it, and neither would it be compensated by anyone, in any way, for its potential losses. Thus, rather than trying to adapt to the Western rules, it makes more sense for Russia's leadership to act entirely at its own discretion, at least within the limits set by their available resources. As for the international (Western) response to their actions, Russian elites believe that they should simply be ignored.

Essentially, this was precisely the Kremlin's position on the issue of Syria. It did the same, except even more explicitly, and even defiantly vis-à-vis the West, in its response to the political crisis in Ukraine and the attempts by Western politicians to find a resolution to this crisis without deference to the Kremlin's position and interests. These attempts were perceived as a particularly painful slight, as an expression of total disrespect for the Russian political elite's expectations about how the Western community of countries should treat Russia— requirements that the elite saw as unquestionably justified by history.[4]

The West, for its part, categorized present-day Russia as a threat to international stability, which was to be removed through various means, namely, political and economic sanctions and, possibly, coercion. Regardless of the specific measures chosen as the West's immediate response to the Kremlin's actions in the Ukrainian crisis, governments and mass media in Western countries offered their publics an unequivocal interpretation of these Russian steps as a challenge to the familiar world order—a challenge that could not be left without a response. This is their long-term assessment, and it seems unlikely to change, even if the Kremlin and the West find some formula for a mutual adjustment of their interests and demands on the issue of Ukraine.

The conflicts that have been shaking the Kremlin's relationship with the global West since 2014 have led to a predictable outcome: in the view of many, Russia has decidedly split from the international community, in its Western definition, likely for the long term. And its ruling circle has decided that a conspicuous isolation or self-isolation of Russia from the West suits them better than attempts to adjust their behavior to the West and its rules. While some observers, both in Russia and in the West, claim that this decision was made by one man—Vladimir Putin—it is hardly possible to deny that these kinds of sentiments are widespread in Russia's ruling circle and within its political class as a whole.

For the same reason, the Kremlin's official adoption of this "new" course in international affairs, first and foremost in the former Soviet regions, did not meet with even muted resistance; in fact, it was received with genuine enthusiasm by most of Russia's elite. The long-standing popular view of Russia as cosmopolitan, closely tied to the West by its business and everyday interests, had turned out to be at odds with reality. Instead, it became clear that the bulk of Russia's administrative and business elite was well aware of the actual source of its affluence and was not ready to risk losing it for the sake of tenuous benefits to be derived from their interactions with the West, whether at the same level as before or even at a more intensive level.

Understandably, the Kremlin's official, public position, which is bound to be somewhat deceitful, refers, as before, to the importance of dialogue, to the need to seek common ground, to the desirability of cooperation and the benefits that it brings to both sides, and so on. Nevertheless, we must lucidly acknowledge that the changes that have occurred in this sphere are very far-reaching. Under the present circumstances, any "return to the early 1990s," when Russia's still embryonic authoritarianism was outwardly ready to accept the prescribed role of a subordinate and externally controlled piece in the big picture of the global order, is unthinkable. For the Kremlin, the state of confrontation with the West and the denial of the role that had been prearranged for it is becoming not merely acceptable but even comfortable. It provides the ruling circle with the opportunity to set up a mobilization-oriented framework of domestic political development, effectively thwarting the protestations by those forces inside Russia that are trying to counteract this situation.

Moreover, by emphasizing in its propaganda that it has been the initiative of the West to punish Russia as a violator of the rules, through the use of economic sanctions, the Kremlin absolves itself of its responsibility for the impending deterioration of economic conditions in Russia, where high consumption levels and, especially, further economic growth depend upon close ties with its global metropole, the West. It is worth noting that the role played by the Ukrainian crisis in the authoritarian regime's turn toward self-isolation from the West should not be overstated. The crisis only provided a convenient pretext for Russia's ruling elite to make a show of its "divorce" from the West. The political and economic preconditions for it had ripened earlier and were merely awaiting for an appropriate occasion to come to the fore and to propel the Kremlin into action. Had this action been taken at a later stage, it might have been less showy but more thorough and irreversible in its impact.

In my view, the economic preconditions for this turn away from the West were more definitive. Namely, the resource export–oriented framework of Russia's economy had exhausted its capacity to serve as the engine of economic development and consumption, not merely in theory but also in practice. This conclusion became a point of consensus among almost all political forces in Russia and was repeated nearly ad nauseam; yet, for quite a while, Russia's elite was not truly and completely aware of what this actually meant. It was only after the 2008–2009 crisis and the evaporation of the hopes for the resurgence of the economic "mini miracle" of the "fat years" (2003–2007) that it became plain to see: the growth that relied upon oil and gas exports was actually petering out, and no new impetus for Russia's economic development could be generated just by intensive connections with the West.

Accordingly, Russia's political elite viewed these ties as an asset of diminishing value, and the possibility of formal and informal sanctions by Western countries was no longer a constraint for the Kremlin. The disappearance of prior benefits from the growth of raw materials exports to leading industrial countries was ascertained as a fact by the bulk of Russia's elite that was not directly involved with these industries. Meanwhile, the opportunities to diversify the range of industries and economic activities specifically through close interactions with Western economies either were nonexistent to begin with or were never seized upon by the ruling circle. As a result of all of these factors, Russia's economic elite never put up any significant resistance when the Kremlin began its turn toward political confrontation with the West at the expense of economic ties both with the West and among the elites themselves.

Evidently, the political prerequisites for this turn were primarily related to the outlook and psychology of the man at the top of the authoritarian hierarchy. Specifically, Vladimir Putin found himself a square peg in a round hole in the club of global chief executives; they did not see him as one of their own, let alone equal to them. They viewed even his very presence in the Group of Eight as a leftover from the Cold War, a consequence of Russia's ownership of a disproportionately large stockpile of nuclear weapons and now out of sync with Russia's far humbler role in the world economy, trade, and investment. Meanwhile, the Russian leader's denial of this situation and his aspirations for a larger role were the source of constant mutual irritation and displeasure. Sooner or later, these feelings were bound to erupt, morphing into tough, intransigent actions.

It is also plain to see that the widespread perception of Russia's top elite as a cosmopolitan group, whose economic interests and personal plans connected it tightly to the West, were also at odds with reality. Even those among Russia's business and political elite who, on a personal level, would like to integrate with the "greater West" felt like disrespected and disavowed waifs there, because of their differences from the Western elite in education, psychology, mind-set, and personal experience. They could never get rid of a certain kind of psychological discomfort, which instinctively produced a feeling of being offended, and even a sense of their own superiority over the representatives of the Western elite, whom they saw as pampered and narrow-minded. Most of Russia's high-ranking officials and businesspeople never managed to secure sources of income and social status in the developed world that would be on a par with what they had at home, nor were they able to escape the feeling that the outside world viewed them with a certain disrespect, as global "provincials" of sorts. Naturally, all this affected their outlook, which was reflected in their inability and unwillingness to put up an earnest resistance when the Kremlin created the impetus for hateful and contemptuous rhetoric toward the West.

In this regard, it was entirely natural that the drive toward isolation from the outside world (a result of the Kremlin's actions, which violated the rules established for it) rapidly accelerated and was far-reaching in its development. It was particularly helped by the fact that the Kremlin's actions were accompanied by territorial acquisitions and the associated upswing in patriotic, pro-government feelings—a politically important gain for the ruling circle. The threats issued by the West in this connection even sparked a certain enthusiasm among the elite, rather than scaring them, because this was viewed as a sort of acknowledgement of their grandeur. The Kremlin could afford to act as it saw fit, without worrying about the "international community." The prospect that Western governments could freeze and seize the foreign assets of Russia's high-ranking officials, particularly those of the uniformed agencies, was only welcomed—both by Putin, their unquestionable leader, who had already been pursuing a policy of "nationalization of the elite," and, one might say, by Russia's population as a whole.

Judging by objective indicators and facts (to the extent that we can), it appears that the upper crust of Russia's government bureaucracy, including its economic officials, was rather unfazed by the Kremlin's proclamation of its willingness to drastically minimize Russia's political and, for the most part, even economic relations with Western countries. In any case, during the period when this turnaround became clearly and unambiguously pronounced, there were no resignations or any visible activities on the part of any government officials that could be interpreted as an attempt to publicly indicate resistance to these policies. There are other trends as well, to be discussed later in this chapter, that reinforce the turn toward isolation from the outside world and, furthermore, that obstruct the path to a potential reversal of these policies. In light of this, there is a high probability that the period of decline in or freezing of the Russian elite's connections with the outside world (or, more precisely, with the outside world's most developed part) will continue for as long as Russia's new authoritarianism continues in its present form.

Still, much will depend upon the dynamics of the Ukrainian crisis. Indeed, an attentive and unbiased analysis of developments in Ukraine shows that, while the internal determinants of this crisis were very significant, one of its primary causes was located outside of Ukraine. Namely, this cause lay in developments in Russia, where the system of peripheral authoritarianism continuously tried to extend its "living space," to spread into former Soviet countries, and to fulfill its desire to rigidly impose upon these countries its own rules and ways of life. This behavior was an inherent element of the ripening and consolidation of this system.

Given the exceptional significance that the tragic events unfolding in Eastern Ukraine since the spring and summer of 2014 hold for Russia's future, as well as the political consequences of the annexation of Crimea, let us digress a bit from the framework and flow of our analysis and take a closer look at the Russian–Ukrainian situation. In terms of their culture and history, Russia, Ukraine, and Belarus belong to the European civilization; the European path is the only practically available path for their further development. There is simply nothing else available to them, provided that these countries want to preserve their statehood in the twenty-first century. Attempts to move in a different direction are a deviation from their natural historical development, as was the Bolshevik experiment of building socialism/communism. The difference between now and then is that, nowadays, the outcome of such an attempt would be even more destructive for the countries that would experiment with it. The special significance of the Ukrainian crisis is that it has been the first large-scale, overt expression of an attempt to deviate from the European path and that it was directly caused by the disruption of the natural process of European-oriented development in the post-Soviet space.

As I mentioned earlier, Russia played the central role in the crisis in Ukraine. By increasingly pursuing "Eurasianist" domestic and foreign policies since the turn of the century, Russia has been stubbornly trying to follow a development direction that is widely characterized as anti-European. In its turn, Russia's refusal to follow the European path, both in its practical actions and at the level of the Kremlin's political rhetoric, means that the post-Soviet space is being torn apart, pulled in different directions. The Ukrainian crisis is a consequence of this, as

Russia tries to pull Ukraine in an anti-European direction instead of moving together with it in the opposite direction.

Meanwhile, relations between society and government in Ukraine were, for quite a while, essentially based upon a certain kind of social contract: Ukrainians were willing to temporarily put up with a regime that was ugly, corrupt, and inefficient, provided that Ukraine continued to move toward Europe. This was the principal hope and dream of a great many people all over Ukraine. Moreover, on the eve of the signing of the treaty on Ukraine's association with the European Union, it was clear that the choice in favor of Europe was not a divisive but rather a consolidating decision for the country, even though the ramifications of this step were not going to be uniformly beneficial for everyone. In the mind-set of the Ukrainians, the choice was starkly clear. It was a choice between a European future (however idealized and oversold it might have been) and the kind of present that no one wanted to live in for long. But the Ukrainian government tore up this social contract. As a result, people felt that they had been cheated and humiliated. They revolted; hence the emergence of the Maidan as a political force.

One driving force in Ukrainian politics and street activism is a regional factor focused, first and foremost, on Western Ukraine—former Galicia (Halychyna and the Lviv region) and Bukovina (the Chernivtsi region). For more than five centuries, these regions were not incorporated into Russia, and the culture and mind-set of their populations are certainly different from those of Eastern and Central Ukrainians. The people from these territories who participated in Kyiv's Maidan were more stubborn and radical than, for example, the Kyivans. And yet, as I will discuss, this was not the most important reason why the situation radicalized.

If the powers that be seek to block the development of a society that is energetic, capable of advancing, and demands serious institutional changes, and if the authorities put a straitjacket on that society in order to suppress it, the change will nonetheless occur. The baby will be born, so to speak, but it will be deformed by these restrictions. Take the rule of Russia's Nicholas II as an example. At the time, Russia's government was detached from society and refused to change. This led to the situation in which the desire of Russia's elite to act in the spirit of its times—to transform the autocracy into a constitutional monarchy and thereby create the necessary conditions for Russia's further development—instead produced the Bolshevik monster.

Today, a hundred years later, Russia's ruling circle is much more avaricious, petty, and vindictive, while also being less educated and cultured than the prerevolutionary autocracy. It views the development of society as a threat to itself and tries to pretend, in an irrational and preposterous manner, that no such development is possible. It restrains society with a stiff straitjacket of restrictions, prohibitions, perversions, and lawlessness, yet, by doing this, it ushers in the birth of yet another social and political monstrosity, whereby Russian politics will be dominated by outright illiterate, populist, and radical people.

Russia's peripheral authoritarianism perceived developments in Ukraine as an assault upon the essence of Russia's existing political system. Yet the Kremlin did not dare to defend the Eurasianist system directly; instead, it proclaimed itself to be a fighter for Russia's interests. It demonstrated this, first, through the illegal annexation of Crimea, which was bound to increase its popularity, and second, through the defense of Russian speakers against Ukrainian nationalists (widely known in Russia as "Banderists," after Stepan Bandera, the leader of one of the most militant nationalist groups in Ukraine during World War II).

Even so, the gist of the actions undertaken by the Kremlin was related less to Crimea (which is just an additional trophy) than to the preservation of the power of the ruling circle in Russia and to the defense of Russia's authoritarian peripheral-type system against an onslaught. (And this was the second such onslaught, at that. The first was the exposure of the fraud perpetrated in the course of Putin's reelection to the presidency in 2004.) This was also the case in the Soviet invasion of Hungary in 1956 and of Czechoslovakia in 1968; these invasions were not about territory but rather were a response to the countries' rise against the authoritarian system of rule. This is precisely why Russia was irreconcilably against Ukraine's association with the EU in any shape or form.

Moreover, Russia's ruling elite set upon the task of stimulating the process of destruction of Ukrainian statehood and proving to the rest of the world that Ukraine in its present borders is a failed state. Ultimately, Russia's ruling elite has been seeking to redraw/partition Ukrainian territory and to chop off Crimea and Eastern and Southern Ukraine so that Russia can take them over, one way or another. This does not have to be accomplished through annexation; instead, it can be achieved through the creation of a "buffer zone," in some shape and form, between Russia and the West. It is conceivable that Western Ukraine and a part of Central Ukraine may then be able to exist as an independent state, and that Russia will even put up with their accession to the EU and possibly even to NATO (depending on how this "operation" turns out and what kind of territorial configuration emerges as a result.)

In any case, the Kremlin's operation, "Ukraine-2014," was aimed at reinforcing the non-European, "Eurasianist" character of the Russian state. It is a state that interprets human rights and international law in its own way, that assumes the role of an adversary of the West, and that ultimately maintains all the principal components of the "sovereign" criminal-oligarchical system of governance created after 1991. In the event that this operation is a success, it is quite possible, and even probable, that its zone will be extended into other former Soviet territories as well.

Regardless of the future course of events, however, Russia's slide toward anti-European policies has already created a novel and toxic environment for all of its neighbors, producing among them a strong desire to distance themselves from it as much as possible. Its persistent promotion of quasi-alternative (in fact, nonexistent) Eurasianist values results in a conspicuous disregard for civil and political rights, in a rejection of the principle of citizens' equality before the law, in a weakening of the separation of powers and the rule of law, in the nurturing of an oligarchical system of property ownership, and in a lack of competition in Russia's politics and economy.

Nearly every country that neighbors Russia has significant pro-European forces that are countering the Kremlin's plans to maintain its tight grip upon these countries. Therefore, by its refusal to move in the European direction, Russia gives rise to an extensive geographic belt of instability. In the near future, Russia has a considerable capacity to generate instability in Ukraine by using its economic leverage (Ukraine's dependence upon Russian markets and energy resources) and by fueling secessionism through infusions of money and media propaganda. Because of this, the prospects of a European future for Russia are among the key issues for Ukraine and for the post-Soviet region as a whole.

Only a shared pan-European vision can be commensurate with Russia's intent while also being capable of exciting its people rather than scaring them off. The concept of a "Greater Europe"—from Lisbon to Vladivostok—undoubtedly holds such a promise. And this is not just lofty rhetoric or hot air. This is a weighty, effective approach, and it is the only practical alternative to both the blind alley of steady decomposition into which Russia's society is being driven today and the "new" but actually old myth about nationalism as the only possible driving force of a liberal revolution.

For Europe (and for Russia and Ukraine as its inherent parts), self-identification with this notion of a Greater Europe and consistent efforts to put it into practice in the economy, in politics, and in military strategy are the only means to survive and to rise to a new, significantly higher level in global affairs and in economic competition with North America and Southeast Asia in the twenty-first century. On its own, Europe will never be able to succeed in this regard—and certainly the Eurasianist Russia that rejects the West and considers it a threat will not.

Overall, Europe can be strong and promising only if the European way of life keeps expanding and continues to transcend its present boundaries. If Europe stops growing and decides that the political definition of Europe is limited by the borders of the former Soviet Union after the accession of the Baltic states to the EU, then such a Europe, deprived of the energy of moving forward, will become increasingly bureaucratic, frozen, and prone to decay. Moreover, Russia and Ukraine, with their cultural and historical experience, their traditions, and their power of creativity, which they have preserved against all odds, can play a positive role in addressing many of the challenges that Europe faces.

RUSSIA AS A "POLE" IN A MULTIPOLAR WORLD: THE NEW IDEOLOGICAL FETISH

As I noted in chapter 3, a classical authoritarian power tends not to be overly concerned with developing an integrated universal ideology; instead, it focuses on control over the resources of financial and administrative power, without seeking to rule the minds and thoughts of the population it governs. It does not pay that much attention to what the population thinks, and when it does, this attention is usually limited to a bunch of platitudes loudly proclaimed as the official ideology—typically along the lines of being on the side of everything that people view as good and being against all evil.

This principle is undoubtedly true when an autocracy is in its formative stage or is at its peak and is confident enough to have no need for an additional prop in the form of a universal and mandatory ideology. This is also the safer course, as the use of such an ideology as a tool of governance carries with it not only potential benefits but also certain complications and risks. Ideologies often invoke deeply held feelings and instincts that are easy to arouse but extremely difficult to control or tame when government interests require it.

Yet, in the section of that chapter titled "In Search of an Ideology," I noted that the period when Russia's present-day authoritarian regime was thriving and exuding self-confidence did not last very long. By approximately 2010, it became plain to see that the prior rapid and tangible growth of Russians' incomes could not be sustained. Simultaneously, the opportunities for the elite to appropriate and distribute a hefty bureaucratic rent reached a hard limit as, in fact, the amounts of this rent stopped growing.

At the same time, the authorities embarked upon a more active pursuit of an additional source of support, in the realm of ideology. Eventually, they discovered it in the conservative valorization of the status quo, which included a quasi-religious veneration of the powers that be; the notion of a "peoplehood," understood as an inseparable bond between the people and its government; and an emphasis upon "traditional values." This ideological mix also included a cult of the princely symbols of national "grandeur," coupled with overconfidence regarding the potency of the widely touted symbiotic relationship between the authorities and the people, as well as xenophobia, with its perception of a hostile international encirclement and a country besieged by its enemies and their minions. By about 2010, all the ingredients of this mix became fairly pronounced and firmly implanted in the style and political content of government-owned and government-oriented media and in the official statements and pronouncements by members of the ruling circle and pro-government cultural figures.

Finally, I have noted that the increasing ideological zeal of Russia's authorities, and their attempts to find an additional source of support through a more aggressive brainwashing of the public, has had two implications. On the one hand, it attests to the fact that the system has already passed the peak of its resilience. It is in the process of losing, or has already lost, its prior confidence that the relatively comfortable, safe strategy of non-ideological control over the situation in the country is sufficient for its purposes. On the other hand, such actions by the authorities are extremely risky, as they awaken and energize forces within society that are capable of causing havoc and that will be quite difficult to keep under control.

Under these circumstances, a natural and rather tempting solution to this quandary is to remake the state in an ideological mold. In such an ideologically defined state, defending, promoting, and asserting the ideology that suits the authorities becomes an item on the government's agenda. Meanwhile, all opinions that are not officially sanctioned are excluded from the range of the acceptable and are effectively suppressed. In other words, the authorities set themselves upon the slippery slope of a transformation of their authoritarian system into a totalitarian one, with all the implications of this change.

These are precisely the trends that, in recent years, have been increasingly infiltrating Russia's political life and, moreover, that have started to turn into a permanent fixture. All the main features of the Kremlin's "new" set of policies have become full-fledged components of the official ideology—even though all the ingredients of its eclectic mix were simply borrowed from various periods of Russia's history, from early medieval autocracy to the Soviet era.[5] They have replaced the residual rhetoric of "transition," with its ritualistic vows of loyalty to the principles of democracy, human rights, and economic freedom. The course toward political isolation from "Western" influence has made these incantations not just unnecessary but even detrimental in terms of mobilizing popular support for the new ideological direction. This is why all the "programmatic" statements and documents that have emanated from the top of the hierarchy of power since about 2015 have already been virtually devoid of any trace of the liberal frame of mind. Instead, they are single-mindedly focused on the notion of a unified and monolithic power, its direct reliance upon the "will of the people" (without any mention of the tools of representative democracy), and the building of relations with the outside world entirely on the Kremlin's own terms and from a position of power.

A huge part of this new ideological framework is the premise that it is the authorities' duty to protect and invigorate traditional values, safeguarding them from potential "corrosion" or dilution by external influences. The propaganda firmly binds these traditional values to Russian ethnicity and Russia's landmass and, further, envisions them as a given (as "primordial foundations") that is not subject to change, rethinking, or even adjustment based on new realities. Essentially, this new ideological construct no longer envisions government as a product of some social bargain but rather views it as the direct expression of the popular or national spirit, the "spirit of the turf," whose raison d'être is to organize Russian resistance to the a priori hostile and alien outside world.

Such a model of government organization and functioning leaves no room for any separation or distribution of power among competing agencies, nor for any mechanism of holding this supreme authority accountable for its actions. At most, what can fit into this construction is a modicum of control, however ineffective, over the activities of the lowest levels of the government machinery, exercised by the population "from below." That is, the authorities may consider cooperating with citizens in holding junior government staff to account, but nothing more.

It is natural that the shift in ideological emphasis necessitated adjustments in the editorial policies of the national TV channels, which have served as the primary tool in the authorities' engagement with public opinion. These channels now began deleting references to the existence of viewpoints different from the official policy, even if those references were critical of these alternate views. And when these viewpoints do get mentioned, they are invariably accompanied by comments about the existence of a "fifth column" in the country, which works to advance foreign interests. Those who represent other ideologies have been reclassified from intellectual schismatics to committed enemies of Russia's national statehood who must be denied even the tiniest place in public and political life. Meanwhile, the intensity of propaganda has been maximized and is now bordering on hysteria. The authorities have been purging all the institutions that have any access to public opinion—from the State Duma to the Chamber of Nongovernmental Representatives under the presidential administration—of "troublemakers" who have used their membership in these agencies to convey their antigovernment opinions to the public.

Simultaneously, the Kremlin upgraded the role of the dominant ideology as the theoretical justification for political and everyday xenophobia as well as for the exceptional importance of state-oriented consciousness among Russians. Prior to that, the notion of the "Russian world"—the worldwide community of Russians, mostly defined by ethnicity, language, and/or affiliation with the Russian Orthodox Church and used as a counterweight to the idea of Russia's multiethnic civic nation—was primarily of interest to nationalistic intellectuals. Now this vision has become not only a part of the official doctrine but also the unofficial basis for the Kremlin's foreign policy strategy in the post-Soviet region, interpreted by government-affiliated ideologists of Russia's political and territorial expansion as an ethnonational state. In essence, if not explicitly, the slogan of "gathering the Russian lands together" and "unifying ethnic Russians" has become the new officially sanctioned idea.

It goes without saying that the rejection of universal values of democracy and human rights has become a major component of this official ideology. The propaganda attributes these notions to the "hostile West," which enables it to manipulate them as it sees fit, if not to deny them outright. Restricting these rights in every possible way, and narrowing them by every means, becomes no longer a violation of the fundamental norms of human coexistence but rather an assertion of the government's natural right to protect Russia's security and distinctiveness, allegedly rooted in national traditions and values. Essentially, this is an affirmation of what was already tried at the beginning of the century under the label of "sovereign democracy," but now it is a component of an already more cohesive official ideological doctrine.

In other words, the ideology spontaneously developed by Russia's post-Soviet authoritarian regime has occupied an expanded role in government and society and has acquired the embryonic shape of an ideology of a Eurasianist state, portrayed as the embodiment of centuries-old Russian polyethnic values. These values allegedly consist of the rejection of individualism and greed and the dissolution of the individual into a distinctive social organism, a symbiotic relationship between the people and the authoritarian power that is imbued with a metaphysical sense inaccessible to average mortals. And this authoritarian power is envisioned as preexisting from the beginning of time and independent of contemporary society, as if detached from any specific individuals in time and space.

Certainly, the elements of such an ideology existed long before present-day Russia's authoritarianism; some of its roots are centuries old. This ideology was shaped as a cohesive whole on the fringe of twentieth-century philosophy. Now Russia's homegrown peripheral authoritarianism has put it to use because, overall, it suits the regime's need for ideological tools of consolidation of its power and its defense against domestic and foreign threats, both real and imagined. Moreover, the Kremlin's sense of its need for such a protection turned out to be so strong that it offset even the evident drawbacks in terms of governance.

Using such an ideology for this specific purpose under Russia's current conditions presents obvious difficulties. First, too many people belonging to large, primarily ethnic minorities begin to experience an indelible sense of ambiguity with regard to their position within the Russian state. Second, some of the institutions inherited from the previous period are now up in the air because of the uncertainty about whether and how they fit in with this new ideology. These institutions include, for example, political parties that had been created within a different framework of political development; the educational system, whose current organization allows for a multiplicity of viewpoints, which is unacceptable under the new ideology; and a few others.

Nevertheless, it appears that Russia's supreme authorities have made their political choice. All subsequent moves will be toward consolidating Russia's government-centered Eurasianism as the basic idea of the Russian state, and currently existing governmental and public agencies and institutions will be adjusted to it. Soon, as with any official state ideology, the Kremlin will have to decide how rigidly it will be applied, and to what practical political purposes. We will find this out in the immediate future.

THE POLITICAL FRAMEWORK OF PUTIN'S RUSSIA: IN PURSUIT OF A PERFECT HIERARCHY

Finally, the third among the authoritarian tendencies listed at the beginning of this chapter has been the drift of the regime toward a highly rigid, vertical framework for its power hierarchy. This became particularly visible during the "Crimean campaign" of 2014 and its immediate aftermath. The gist of this development is that the "Putin system" of rule seeks to get rid of the elements of political competition that are alien to it and out of place in today's Russia, as well as of any alternative sources of power in the country. In chapter 3, I discussed the fact that today's authoritarian regime grew out of the eclectic realities of post-Soviet transition. Its growth and consolidation were the outcome of a lengthy, largely spontaneous and unreflective search for a political framework that would articulate and protect the interests of the new ruling class—the post-Soviet *nomenklatura*.

Naturally, this search was neither simple nor unidirectional. The twists, turns, and breaking points associated with this search became especially visible at certain distinctive moments of Russia's post-Soviet history. To begin with, these were the first years after the collapse of the Soviet system, years that ended with the notorious events of the fall of 1993—the disbanding of the legislature by President Boris Yeltsin, followed by violent confrontation in the streets of Moscow. The political framework that was designed in the wake of these events was fundamentally new—the framework of a presidential (or, according to some experts, superpresidential) republic.

The second of these moments was the presidential election campaign of 1996, when the ruling circle that was then in power abandoned, for the first time, the idea of having truly competitive elections. Yet another turning point was in 1999, when that ruling circle for the first time resorted to a behind-the-scenes transfer of power and Boris Yeltsin, the leader of the ruling circle, who was physically unfit to continue his duties as president, effectively appointed his official successor to the "throne," Vladimir Putin. Then, in the beginning of the next decade, the Kremlin began setting up what is known in Russia as the "vertical of power," the system of full command from above, from the head of state down through the whole chain of government, from the federal level to the local level and including the powers of legislature and law enforcement. The gist of this process was the curbing of autonomous political activity of any kind in Russia's regions and political parties.

In 2012–2013, the Kremlin reinstated gubernatorial elections, though in a truncated form, and somewhat relaxed the restrictions on the activities of Russia's political parties. This seemed to signal a certain departure from the mainstream policy of curtailing political competition. Yet, by the beginning of 2014, the political climate in the country had deteriorated as never before: the authorities questioned the very principle of political pluralism, and the boundaries between opposition work and political subversion became completely blurred in the official media and rhetoric.

What was so distinctive about the situation and the trends in this area that became plain to see in early 2014? First, at the time, the political profiles of the officially ruling political party (United Russia) and those opposition parties that were represented in the Duma (the Communists, the Liberal Democrats, and Fair Russia) became completely indistinguishable from one another. The proceedings of the legislature were now entirely devoid of any critique of Putin, not only in response to his actions in the Ukrainian crisis but also on any other issue. This change could not be explained by nationwide patriotic fervor, as some tried to do, nor by the claim that it would have been inappropriate to criticize the supreme authority at that critically important and momentous time. If political parties are competing with each other and represent different groups within the elite, then subtle and not-so-subtle differences in their approaches to the most important political issues of the day never disappear completely, even in the face of an actual foreign threat.

What is there to say about conditions if there are no obvious indicators that such threats are getting stronger or more imminent than before, or when survival of the state is much more dependent upon the character and substance of the authorities' response to domestic challenges? In such a situation, the touching unanimity between the government and the official opposition reveals something else: either all of these political parties are no more than different subsidiaries of the same ruling circle and are essentially in the service of one set of interests or, just as likely, the ruling circle has decided that intra-elite disagreements may present an unacceptable danger to them and should, at the very least, be pushed deep down below the surface and not be allowed to show up in public, even in the gentle form of parliamentary debates.

Whatever the case, Russia's federal representative bodies, starting with the State Duma, have by now become part and parcel of a monolithic authoritarian rule that does not permit even the slightest opportunity for organized political alternatives to crystallize within the framework of political legality. The only way to rule out such a possibility while still having multiple political parties is by eliminating anything that even remotely suggests that these parliamentary parties may actually represent alternatives to the powers that be—or by eliminating the multiparty system as such. Evidently, the ruling circle has selected the first of these two paths, employing their relations with the bosses of these "opposition" parties and their extensive ability to influence them with either sticks or carrots. This is also related to the intense ideological hardening of the regime, its drift toward ideological totalitarianism, which I characterized earlier. The very presence of an official ideology that is a mandatory article of faith for anyone who does not want to be listed among the traitors and the enemies of the state implies political unity and the absence of entities that might offer themselves as alternatives to the powers that be.

Of course, in this situation, parliamentary elections are becoming entirely devoid of any practical sense. In the preceding period, the ruling circle viewed such elections as a super-representative opinion poll, used to legitimize the role and the status of the country's unquestionable leader. Now, given the lack of any distinguishable differences among the parties (apart from their leaders' names), holding elections does not make sense even as an opinion poll. They either become a farce, a show closely following a predetermined script, or they get abolished altogether. Time will tell which of these two paths will be selected by Russia's authorities; most likely it will be decided ad hoc, depending on the context. Yet, however it ends up, under the conditions of today's Russia, parliamentary elections, being an alien element in a totalitarian or semitotalitarian system, appear to be doomed to extinction.

A second trend that has emerged since 2014 is the consolidation of the ruling circle's economic interests, with drastic curbs on economic lobbying. In the first decade of the new century, there were several distinguishable subgroups within Russia's ruling class, each oriented toward its own sector and industry focus, from the resource industries and large-scale infrastructure projects to manufacturing and even the technologically advanced clusters of the economy. There was also a separate group of the elite that was betting on the development of modern finance (or, in their own words, "the transformation of Moscow into an international financial center"). On top of that, there were subgroups that represented diverse regional interests and priorities, such as those who emphasized the need for an accelerated development of Russia's Far East, those who lobbied for the utilization of Arctic resources, and so on.

These groups worked to produce some theoretical justification for their activities, and visions of economic and social development that were distinguishable from one another. While some of them stressed the need to concentrate financial resources and investment activities in the government's hands and to implement the megaprojects that had been prepared for either existing or projected government-owned corporations, other groups emphasized the need to reduce the tax burden on businesses and to incentivize primarily small and medium-size entrepreneurship. There was a blueprint for developing Russia into an "energy superpower"; this was countered by a plan for "modernization-oriented growth" that would rely upon the high-tech clusters of the economy.

These various groups and currents also had different views about the role of foreign capital in Russia.

The arguments and debates between the proponents and the opponents of individual projects and economic development plans filled the pages and the airwaves of mass media. They were also reflected in behind-the-scenes clashes among various expert groups who were fighting for a benevolent attitude from the Kremlin and for access to additional sources of influence and money. Eventually, these currents of lobbying and economic thought even acquired certain institutionalized forms, such as various councils and associations that had the ability to convey and defend the collective interests of their specific groups.

Granted, this was not quite the same as political competition in its traditional sense; yet, undoubtedly, the rivalry among lobbyists and interest groups, each vying for a larger share of the financial and administrative pie, also involved some elements of a political contest. Even given the tight restrictions under which they operated, these groups nevertheless were increasing the flexibility of the system and providing it with a feedback mechanism, which to some extent enabled it to adjust in response to the changing challenges.

Nowadays, the increasing rigidity of Russia's political framework has affected these aspects as well. Under budgetary constraints, reinforced by the drastic decline in economic efficiency and the rising costs incurred by self-isolation, the wiggle room that generates competition among economic interests has narrowed. Putin's "new course" imparts a peremptory style to the decisions it makes about the industrial and geographic priorities of its economic policy, thus making lobbying efforts largely meaningless. Meanwhile, the new ideological "braces," as they are called by the media, have drastically diminished the value and the worth of any intellectual support for competing economic interests. This is exacerbated by the trend toward an even greater concentration of decision-making power in the hands of one individual—Vladimir Putin—who, on top of that, is increasingly impatient with those who disagree with him or raise any objections to his viewpoints and is increasingly judgmental in his statements about individuals and groups who express their discontent with developments in the country. As a result, even this modicum of competition is viewed as a threat and becomes a target for coercive pressure.

A final trend is the rejection of the horizontal ties between the elements of this political system and the outside world. The policy of self-isolation implies that any international contacts with individual agencies that do not directly involve the people at the top of the pyramid of power are becoming not just a nuisance but even a potentially dangerous activity. This affects not only nongovernmental organizations and semigovernmental entities (including academic, analytical, cultural, educational, and charitable institutions) but also official agencies of the government, such as regional governments, territorial associations, administrations of local and other units subject to special economic regulations, and the like.

As a result, the overall amount of international contact inevitably begins to shrink, and this also indirectly constrains the economic activities of foreign players or of business entities with foreign participation on Russia's territory. The policy of attracting foreign capital is being replaced with indifference or even hostility to it on the part of the authorities. While Russia is not yet being shut off from the outside world, it is a significant step in this direction and may be fraught with grave implications for the long haul. (At present, this development is still at a very early stage, but some of its obvious indicators are already discoverable and can be evaluated.)

In this regard, the government's surveillance of its citizens' foreign contacts will not focus only on civic activists and roaming oppositionists. It also will target individuals from the ranks of the seemingly docile bureaucracy who have opportunities for unrestrained contacts with the outside world and are able to acquire some kind of assets abroad. Just a few years ago, the bureaucracy appeared to be permanently entitled to such "unpatriotic" behavior; nowadays, this entitlement is being questioned by the people at the top of government hierarchy. Thus, the elite have serious reasons to believe that the new policies aimed at their cosmopolitan members are being introduced in earnest and for the long haul. It is easy for the Kremlin to pivot the campaign of "de-offshorization," or repatriation of Russians' assets from the tax havens, and of the "nationalization of the elite" precisely toward cutting off any independent contacts of government officials with the outside world. And there already are indications that a full-fledged movement in this direction, greatly facilitated by US and UK sanctions, is already under way.

FROM PERIPHERAL TO PAROCHIAL: THE TRAJECTORY OF AN AUTHORITARIAN REGIME

In the previous chapters, I sought to show that authoritarianism as a political system is essentially an unavoidable or nearly unavoidable result of the domination of a peripheral-type capitalism in the country. The reason for this is that, being peripheral, this type of capitalism relies upon a narrow range of rather unsophisticated resources and, therefore, by its very nature, does not generate sufficient prerequisites for a full-fledged functioning of the institutions of political competition. The types of resources that it relies upon may include the raw materials that are of interest to the countries of the core of global capitalism, or it may be an abundant, cheap workforce or the opportunity to minimize material and transportation costs.

Whatever the case, such a country has few opportunities to integrate into the economy of world capitalism, and these opportunities are rather simple and plain to see. Therefore, the section of the ruling stratum that occupies the key positions of executive power can easily dominate and monopolize these opportunities. This group of power holders inevitably brings under its control existing as well as emerging economic entities, and this, in turn, undermines the very possibility of an open and relatively fair competition among various political forces and groups. Thus, the ruling circle suffocates the alternative to its rule through economic means, by depriving the alternative of the opportunity to acquire an autonomous and legally tenable material foundation. No genuine political competition is feasible in a system in which all the main economic resources are under the control of a single group of people.

This pattern applies to all countries of the global periphery, though with certain country-specific variations, and it is the case even if the authorities in these countries officially affirm the existence of political freedoms, multiple political parties, the role of elections, and everything else that is conventionally viewed as an indicator of a political democracy. In its basic traits, the Russian variation of such a system confirms the validity of this relationship, but it is complicated by the oligarchical structure of the ownership of large-scale economic assets as well as by the conditional—that is, revocable—character of this ownership, which was inherent in the loans-for-shares auctions of the mid-1990s and in other forms of arbitrary redistribution of wealth in post-Soviet Russia.

Regardless of these differences, however, a peripheral capitalism is very hard to transform politically in the direction of a competition-based system and the rule of law. Thus, within such a system, there typically is no room to secure funding for public projects independently of the ruling circle—whether for political parties, for civic organizations, or for dependable, free mass media that would reflect a broad spectrum of professionally credible opinions on the salient issues of the day. Within this framework, it is impossible to set up the legal system in such a way that it does not depend upon the will of a single group of power holders occupying the key positions in the executive branch and thus having the power to steer the major flows of financial and other material resources whichever way they want. In such a society, it becomes impossible to determine a development direction through interaction among different interest groups (which, after all, is the real gist of political democracy). Instead, the country's future is shaped by the unfettered dominance of individual whims and by the selfish pursuits and beliefs of a narrow circle of people with a monopolistic grip on power and on the management of large-scale economic assets.

On the other hand, the authoritarianism that develops in the countries of the global periphery also has a peripheral character in its relation to the core of the present-day world. While such a regime has enormous power to control its host society, it trails behind world leaders in international affairs and is incapable of influencing either global development or its own.

At the same time, the condition of any given society and state is not determined solely by its economy and its position in the world economic system. Other significant factors include political will, the state of the elite (or even their very existence), and the integrity of the national consciousness and its dominant ideological concepts. Otherwise, history would not contain examples of countries and societies that managed to make a breakthrough and move up to a higher orbit in their trajectory, substantially closer to the center of global development. No society is ever a priori doomed to eternal backwardness and to always being on the remote periphery of the world economy and the global community. In the same way, the fact that a given country has gained a place in the core of this world economy is no guarantee that it will always remain there.

Granted, changing one's fortune requires deliberate and persistent effort. This is just as true for countries and peoples as it is true for individuals. To make a transition from the periphery to the center requires not only time and resources but also intellect, knowledge, and maneuverability. It requires the ability to find one's way out of unfavorable situations and even out of situations in which a loss cannot be avoided, including by playing upon the tensions among one's competitors and upon their weaknesses.

It is incumbent upon society's elite to lead the country along this path. Such an elite must be not just educated but also energetic, goal-oriented, and capable of confronting the most inert, reactionary part of its own society and of prevailing in this conflict. And for this, in turn, such an elite must be equipped with a fitting ideology. They must aspire to be an active participant in the international struggle for economic and technological leadership, without fearing competition, without expecting others to give them a break or an entitlement, and certainly without expecting to be given the coveted high status without any effort on their part. This elite must realize that, in the harsh world of international competition, neither past achievements (whether real or imaginary) nor self-proclaimed historical grandeur nor claims to a leadership role without underlying practical capabilities and resources counts. Furthermore, the elite must be unafraid of admitting their own mistakes or, for the sake of getting things done, of playing the role of a junior partner that cannot impose its own views and understanding of the situation upon the key players in world politics.

On the other hand, if the elite turn out to be devoid of all such characteristics, then it becomes virtually impossible to close even some of the gap separating it from the center of the world system. In this instance, the impulse to avoid taking part in this struggle, by hiding behind the slogan of self-sufficiency and an a priori spiritual superiority, becomes a natural response. And then the condition of being peripheral—which by itself is not incompatible with pursuing the goal of gradually overcoming this condition—turns into parochialism.

The distinctive feature of this parochialism is a pronounced reluctance to change one's position on the global order of things, as well as the conviction that the familiar status quo and the concomitant way of life are the best options that are realistically possible. The media start portraying poverty as beneficial and describing stagnation—defined as a confidence-instilling stability, inertness, and the unwillingness to change—as fidelity to tradition. And the sense of one's greatness becomes an a priori given that requires no validation through practical achievements or through victories in a competitive race. From this point of view, and taking into account everything that followed from the crisis over Ukraine-2014, including the annexation of Crimea and the hybrid war in Eastern Ukraine, we need to add some further precision to the characterization of Russia's authoritarianism as peripheral.

First of all, it has to be said that peripheral is indeed what Russia's authoritarianism continues to be, in spite of its regular declarations about its exceptionalism, its sovereignty, and its principle of autonomy in relation to the rest of the world. By rejecting the possibility of taking part in the system of global governance, even if as a second-tier player, Russia validates its peripheral character. Though it refuses to play a role as even a secondary participant in managing world affairs, it nonetheless remains part and parcel of these affairs, but it occupies a passive position. Now, instead of Russia having some degree of influence in resolving international problems, these problems will be resolved without Russia at the table and without taking its interests into account.

At the same time, by insulating Russia from the global capitalist core—in political and, therefore, in economic terms—its authoritarianism transforms itself into a parochial regime. From being on the outskirts of a large metropolis, with every opportunity to become a part of it and thus to gain a voice in its governance system, this regime tries to turn itself into an obscure village, about which the metropolis essentially couldn't care less.

Granted, no one will interfere with the regime's distinctive way of life within this village, which is based on its own mental structure—even if this means the way of life and the mores of many centuries ago, where might makes right, where the weaker members of society have no rights at all, and where anything that moves or even stirs without permission from the powers that be gets suppressed. But neither will anyone let this regime interfere with the life of the global city from now on, whether directly or not, whether by economic coercion or by armed force—if the regime even manages to maintain such a force.

Indeed, the authoritarian regime that is taking shape in today's Russia is not just a peripheral-type but also a parochial one. It exults in its peripheral position and strives to stabilize it for the sake of maintaining power in the hands of the currently ruling group. It takes the territory under its control out of the global developmental process while consciously pitting itself against the forces of global governance and trumpeting its disagreement with the principles on which this governance was built after World War II. One such principle is the principle of the ladder of power and responsibility, according to which anyone's claims to be a force that shapes the rules of international behavior must be backed up by the economic, financial, and organizational capabilities that match this role.

Thus, the path toward upgrading one's status within the system of global governance lies precisely in building up these capabilities instead of ditching the rules because they have been set up by someone else. After all, these rules, which had taken a more or less steady form by the end of the twentieth century, emerged as the outcome and the product of numerous wars waged over many centuries by European powers striving to validate their respective exceptionalisms. These wars crushed tens of millions of human lives and destroyed untold fruits of their labor. And this unwritten code of rules, soaked in human blood, will not be amended to fit the ambitions and the notions of justice held by a single national leader, or even a group of such leaders who are unhappy with their present status in the world community.

A parochial authoritarianism in its Russian avatar acts differently; it seeks to demonstrate to the entire world its own, different rules of existence. It is narrow-mindedly confident that this is just the way everything has worked, everywhere, from time immemorial to our days and into the foreseeable future. It aspires to maintain these rules unconditionally within its domain, whose boundaries it arbitrarily redefines as it sees fit. In our specific case, the "Russian world" is just a euphemistic name for a province that includes Russia's full expanse throughout its history. However, in practice it is not feasible to make these rules "legit" on a global scale.

Granted, Russia has considerable military capability, especially taking its nuclear stockpiles into account. Yet its economic capabilities are extremely limited, regardless of its huge territory and abundant natural resources (which do not necessarily or always provide an economic advantage to their owners). At present, moreover, the use of so-called soft or smart power—the power that capitalizes upon society's cultural and intellectual resources—is out of the question for Russia. In this regard, the global periphery is never able to compete with the center, just as a village cannot compete with a city and an area of massive impoverishment cannot compete with a consumer society. Finally, the periphery's propaganda is ineffective, even if the media tools that it uses are up to date. This propaganda is not in the least capable of defining a message in the global media mainstream and it therefore turns into a senseless waste of already scarce resources, squandered upon building castles in the air and fooling one's own population.

The outcome of all these efforts isn't difficult to predict. The logic of the development of a parochial authoritarianism drives it further and further from global politics, toward self-isolation, toward dealing solely with itself, with a clear-cut prospect of a collapse through implosion. Objectively speaking, moving off of this path is a necessity not only for Russia's society as a whole but also for its political class—and even for the authoritarian regime itself, whose lot will be quite unenviable if the ongoing trends continue.

And the key question, the answer to which will determine our future, is the following: Will Russia's political elite and intellectual class be able to find and mobilize its internal power to turn these currently dominant trends around, to try to put the country's trajectory back into the global context, to find a worthy place and a future for Russia there?

THE NEW CAST OF RUSSIA'S AUTHORITARIANISM

Taken together, the trends that I have described have been shaping the new look of Russia's authoritarianism. Its form, here and now, is a logical extension of its preexisting features, but these features are today of a different caliber, due to the hardened external conditions in Russia, the first and foremost being the narrowing range of economic opportunities. In its turn, this shrinking of opportunities was an unavoidable outcome of the peripheral character of Russia's capitalism. The overall slowdown of the growth of the world economy, and the increasingly pronounced distancing of its core from industries and areas of economic activity that had been traditional for it, have complicated the functioning of the economies of the capitalist periphery, including the Russian economy. These economies have no opportunity and no resources to reorient themselves toward the industries that provide more dynamism and a better return on their expenditures. As a result, they are becoming less efficient and are facing a decline in revenues and in capabilities—as well as growing dissatisfaction on the part of the most energetic and ambitious strata of society. These people either begin to look for employment opportunities abroad, on a mass scale, or they express their discontent in whatever ways they can.

Furthermore, the growing problems and constraints in the global economy result in fewer opportunities to provide the requisite conditions for economic prosperity for every country. Hence, the stronger players on the world economic stage are bound to think less about the condition of the periphery of global business and to pay less attention to its interests in world politics and international affairs. In Russia's case, these changes are especially painful to endure, because its national elite thinks of itself as having a more important role and place than they are given by the outside world. World leaders get annoyed by Russia's elite, who loudly claim more influence and rewards than they are able to secure. These leaders feel that Putin is trying to violate the implicit rules of the game (and, with the annexation of Crimea, is just doing whatever he wants, without regard for anybody else). This, in turn, adds insult to injury and leads to even more negative reactions.

Essentially, all this was bound to produce the outcome that we see—instead of gradually converging toward the Western political mainstream, Russia's post-Soviet autocracy has evolved toward closing in upon itself and strengthening its totalitarian features. Let me make it clear, though, that, in the present context, "convergence" does not mean the elimination of differences, let alone the subordination of one's behavior to the interests of a more powerful party. The similarity of political systems based upon internal political competition certainly does not eliminate international competition. Those who speak of the need for a "European path" or a "European choice" for Russia (or at least those among them who truly care for the future of Russia and its people) are well aware of the inevitability of such competition. Thus, when their accusers say that proponents of the European path are going to knuckle under to the West or to the United States, this is nothing but a propagandistic lie.

If we take an unbiased, impartial look at world politics, we notice that the competition among the countries within the global capitalist core is more intense than the competition between the core countries and the global periphery. This is like the animal world, where competition within the same species is far more acute than competition between different species.

Individual companies and their groups tussle with each other over markets, and thus over the promise of future big revenues, more fiercely than did medieval princes fighting over new territories that they sought to utilize and to plunder. The frenzy and the scale of plotting, as well as the pressure, arm-twisting, and resources expended in this economic warfare, are such that many of the wars waged over the past centuries look like Boy Scouts' games in comparison.

And certainly, had Russia been able to accomplish a historic leap from the global semiperiphery (where it belonged at the peak of the Soviet period) into the core of global capitalism, its relations with the other parts of this core would not have been tranquil by any means. Yes, Russia would have had to give consideration to the stronger powers and to yield to them on a number of issues. But, at the same time, Russia would have been able to elbow its way among competing powers and into those areas where it might amass a prevailing concentration of resources; it would have been able to build coalitions, to plot intrigues if needed, and to achieve its goals. As a result, it would have been able to grow not just in relative but also in absolute terms, thus raising its status in the global pecking order of wealth, power, and influence.

Unfortunately, history turned in such a way that Russia lost this opportunity for the long haul. Nothing that has happened so far is truly irreversible, and yet, once the steamroller has accelerated to a certain speed, it is hard to stop, especially if the driver has no intention of doing so and, quite the contrary, is thrilled to see everybody else freaking out and running for cover.

Nonetheless, a steamroller is only good for what it is designed to do: to pave over everything on its path. It is not for road racing or for honing survival skills. In the global race of industrial, postindustrial, and simply modern economies, authoritarian regimes are bound to lose over the long haul—unless they begin to evolve in the direction of advanced, competition-based systems that are equipped with the tools needed to identify and achieve collective societal goals, to ensure "positive selection" of talent in public service, to self-adjust, and to safeguard against foolishness and major blunders with long-term repercussions. However, Russia's political system is not only *not* moving in this direction but is in fact drifting the opposite way.

These days, many people are saying that Russia has reverted to Soviet times, meaning the later part of the Soviet period, the so-called age of stagnation from the late 1960s to the early 1980s, under Leonid Brezhnev. Others are saying that in fact the Soviet era never ended in Russia. However, this isn't true. The present-day situation in Russia is not a return to the period before perestroika. Rather, it is an attempt by the authorities to leapfrog even further back in history, into Russia's remote past, by juxtaposing it with the European—or, as we tend to say these days, the Western—world in a contrived, vulgar, and manipulative manner. This is the undoing of what has been achieved in every direction of the country's development, from modern public institutions and the organization of its economic life to culture, education, and ideology.

This is nothing but an attempt to step aside from the actual struggle for Russia's place under the sun, to dodge this struggle by indulging in the elite's weaknesses, fears, and illusory dreams about building its own "Russian civilization." It is an attempt to hide from actual problems and from having to look for rational and sustainable solutions for them. The elite try to escape from this by freezing all development in society and supplanting it with the pointless pursuit of nonexistent or fake mental constructs. This is an irresponsible attempt to distract the public from actual present risks by warning of bogus "mortal dangers," and it shows an equally irresponsible willingness to endanger the future of Russia's statehood in its present shape and boundaries. Finally, it is an explicit attempt to make the territory of a huge country, which is not at all devoid of any promise, into a global wasteland with no prospects of becoming one of the actual world leaders of the twenty-first century.

How long will they continue this insanity, this dangerous game in which the fate of the country and its people is at stake? The future is fickle, and at present it is impossible to give a definitive answer to this question. Certainly, it will depend to a significant extent upon the external environment, that is, upon the behavior of other international actors. Regardless, the duty of all healthy political forces in Russia is to make an effort to develop and to put forward a realistic alternative, a truly practical plan to overcome the present crisis. If necessary, this plan may need to be imposed upon Russia's fearful and disoriented political elite, which may have to be forced to fulfill its responsibilities toward the country and its people.

5

IN LIEU OF A CONCLUSION

All the actual and potential dangers emanating from Russia's current political regime amount to a tragic grotesque, from the standpoint of historical development. The political system of present-day Russia is the expression and embodiment of the mind-set of the group of people that have been ruling it for more than twenty years. This mind-set is virtually devoid of any serious ideological frameworks of analysis, has no bedrock values beyond individual wants, and worships personal consumption and enrichment. The ruling group tries to give an ideological twist to its policies, of a kind that appeals to the most basic clannish, tribal instincts of a premodern type and to the subconscious fear of the outside world.

Yet this group actually rejects all those values that have a societal dimension and that extend beyond the horizon of individual physical existence. In the minds of its members, maximizing personal satisfaction by taking advantage of their resources of power and influence and by asserting their superiority over those who are weaker and socially vulnerable invariably prevails over the long-term interests of the body of citizens that make up today's Russia. And, paradoxical as it may be, this means that the ruling group welcomes and approves of the trend of Russia's population becoming less sophisticated in their ways of thinking and in their practices, in the organization and the content of their involvement with one another.

In other words, this political system maximizes the demodernization and destruction of society and minimizes everything that imparts substantive meaning, ethics, grace, and constructive development. In essence, it is a variety of a political postmodernism of sorts. It supplants meaning with shiny objects and symbols that affect the subconscious and are not intended to be thought through or analyzed in relation to other concepts. In this regard, it is telling that the present-day insignia of the Russian state eclectically combines the coat of arms of the imperial Russia, the Soviet-era anthem, and the "democratic" flag. Essentially, this is a senseless mix of disparate historical cues. And, in themselves, these symbols belong entirely to the past, which is yet another illustration of the congenital inability of this "Putin system" to solve the problems of Russia's present and future. Instead, these problems are being cold-bloodedly pushed aside—not even to the back burner but all the way to the bottom of the agenda.

Not that this political postmodernism is a uniquely Russian phenomenon. It is burgeoning in plain sight everywhere, even in the most politically "advanced" nations and societies. Yet it arguably takes the most grotesque forms in Russia, due to the distinctive characteristics of the peripheral mind-set of Russia's elite. And this, I believe, is one of its fundamental differences from the totalitarian systems of the past century. Neither the Nazi regime in Germany nor the Soviet system in Russia were grotesque or postmodern. Each of them was earnest in its attempts to impose upon the entire world its own consistent vision of the gist of social relationships, in its own ways. In Nazi Germany, these relationships were reduced to ethnicity and race, while in Soviet ideology they were determined by socioeconomic class. Each system generated a set of functional institutions that were tasked with putting their respective vision into practice.

Moreover, their efforts in this direction were systematic and on a grand scale. And essentially these systems were bound to end as they did, because in the past century the entire world lived and operated within real-life rather than postmodern frames of reference. Thus, one of them, the Nazi regime, was physically beaten as a result of its aggression in trying to expand beyond the confines of Germany. And, in the 1980s, the Soviet system, which was also quite dangerous, was compelled by internal reasons to drastically alter the course of development that was inherent to it.

The situation with Russia's current political system is different. It is grotesque because it feeds off its own past without creating anything new, except for stereotypes intended for mass consumption and slogans devoid of substantive content. Russia's present-day peripheral capitalism is rooted in the Soviet legacy, in combination with the so-called reforms of the 1990s, which did not create any of the institutions necessary for contemporary life. Neither the rule of law as such nor a comprehensive legal system nor a genuine right to private property ownership emerged during this period. All of this and many other items that were of vital necessity for Russia were supplanted with fakes—fake political competition, fake elections, fake political parties, fake parliament, fake law and order, and so on.

But real life abhors a power vacuum. And this vacuum was filled with powerful, real-life institutions that emerged in the place of those that were missing, such as corruption, relations outside of the legal framework and based on implicit "understandings," the cult of the strongman, the Kremlin's "manual control" over routine operations of the government, and the like.

Russia certainly has institutions in their classical sense, as elements of the system of governance and self-regulation of society. But the thrust of these institutions is demodernizing, leading to Russia's irreversible backsliding vis-à-vis the developed world, as it becomes ever more old-fashioned, as well as to the decay and ultimately the breakdown of Russian society. In other words, Russia's present-day peripheral authoritarianism is not a "transitional" one but rather is headed toward a dead end of demodernization. Most importantly, its built-in characteristics—first and foremost the lack of change at the top of the power hierarchy and the absence of alternatives to the ruling group—deprive it of the internal tools and the driving forces required for self-adjustment to realities and for the pursuit of responses to external challenges.

Therefore, I agree with those who believe that this regime is doomed, that it will not be able to find appropriate forms and ways to adjust to realities—unless, of course, these realities themselves are altered in ways that would be catastrophic for the world. If the world succeeds in identifying a path toward sustainable growth in peace and security, and if it avoids sinking into economic chaos and military conflicts, then the new generation of Russia's political class—those who are now in their twenties and thirties—will not be able to preserve and maintain Russia's political system in its current shape without exposing the country to the threat of collapse and destruction.

The risk of such a turn of events is very real. Russia's present political system has already produced some tragic outcomes by putting the country on the brink of a full-scale bloody war. The system is again spinning in the vicious circle whereby its propaganda stokes the fears of an external threat and thereby actually becomes a self-fulfilling prophecy by generating or strengthening these threats. Meanwhile, its overkill in terms of military buildup contributes to the decay of the foundations of Russia's economy and thus does not strengthen but actually reduces Russia's practical capabilities to withstand domestic and foreign threats to its security. Thus, the tragic farce is gradually morphing into an actual tragedy for the country and its society.

To sum up, the system of peripheral authoritarianism in Russia does not simply demonstrate its incapacity to accomplish Russia's foremost task in the twenty-first century, which is to close the gap between Russia and the developed world. In broader terms, it also threatens the very existence of the country in its present shape. It makes Russia an easy prey for all kinds of extremists, political plunderers, and organized crime groups that may transform the state into an empty shell, unable to perform even its most basic functions. What looms on the horizon under such a scenario is anybody's guess.

Is there a way out of this ongoing tragic farce, for Russia to move instead in the direction of modernization and development? This remains an open question, but I believe we must try to find the answer.

AFTERWORD

2018 and the Imperative for Change

About four years have passed since the first edition of this book was written and first published in Russian. Looking back, I can see that its main ideas are still valid and actual, despite changes in Russian life and the political system. Some of the judgments I made back then may look too cautious in light of the realities of 2018; some, on the contrary, may seem premature. But on the whole the situation seems to be progressing (or maybe "regressing" would be a better word) roughly along the lines described in this book. The Russian political system is increasingly developing all the symptoms and features of an anti-mainstream, retrograde authoritarianism that is indifferent to the long-term consequences of its rule, such as stumbling economic growth, outflow of intellect and capital, waste of valuable resources, burgeoning corruption, the oppressive atmosphere of militaristic and xenophobic propaganda, and so on.

Nor have I changed my mind about the reasons why this system has evolved over the years of postcommunist "transition" and has survived in spite of worsening overall conditions. I still believe that the specific type of capitalism that resulted from flawed and unsuccessful attempts to remold the Soviet economy after the system of arbitrary centralized planning collapsed in the late 1980s gradually developed a political system to match. This specific type of capitalism rests upon a rather simple economy based on the development and export of natural resources, the domination of large public and quasi-private corporations—managed by government-appointed managers and proxy owners dependent on the goodwill of the highest authorities—and on the capability of the top bureaucracy to extract and distribute various types of rent income resulting from administrative and direct control over major resources. For such a model, autocratic rule seems to be the only political solution, and that is exactly what happened to postcommunist Russia. In the 1990s and 2000s, the state transitioned from bogus competitive democracy to mature autocracy with unconstrained power for the supreme leader to command all levels and areas of government and to distribute privileges among various layers of bureaucracy.

Because it corresponded to Russia's newly acquired position on the periphery of the world (capitalist) economy, I called the system a "peripheral" system, referring to both its economy and its political design. What I meant was that the political system featured the interrelation between marked features of a peripheral economy—which didn't contain built-in mechanisms to modernize competitiveness or to capture new markets through diversified innovations—and a retrograde autocracy that relied on inert bureaucracy and public employees rather than dynamic private business. Control of the proceeds from the export of oil, gas, and other resources in the era of high and rising world prices for these resources made it completely unnecessary for the top authorities to care about nurturing an alternative tax base to be imposed on booming private business activities. Indeed, private business would inevitably have brought about an uncontrollable flow of private funds to be used for political lobbying and the sponsoring of alternative political groups. Instead, export proceeds and indirect taxes from transactions involving resources were used to establish an essentially antidemocratic and anti-modernizing coalition of beneficiaries of a patronage autocracy. A system of "feeding" large social groups and local communities through a vertical chain of distribution of funds in the name of the "national leader" made it possible to secure popular support for, or at least indifference to, the authorities' suppression of dissenting groups and their attempts to build political opposition.

At the same time, the lack of an incentive to connect with competitive Western markets for sophisticated products and related services made it possible to isolate the country from foreign influences or attempts at political control. This enabled the authorities to protect authoritarian rule by erecting ideological walls through overt propaganda about Russia's exceptionalism and about the need to defend national values and sovereignty from hostile foreign agents and their collaborators inside Russia, who were trying to break the tie between a "sovereign" ruler and his people. The old trick of identifying antigovernment actions and feelings as anti-Russian and subversive of national statehood was used to its utmost, with no efforts spared and no opportunity lost to convince people of the need to support and defend their rulers from hostile attitudes, attacks, or criticism. Relations with the outside world came to be viewed as basically the age-old war between good and evil, with "them" representing evil and "us" the good, who are intentionally slandered or misinterpreted. This picture leaves absolutely no room for even well-intended dissent, let alone competition for power, thus cementing the political construction erected by the autocratic regime.

Nevertheless, I felt there was still some room for history to make corrections or even considerable alterations to this scenario.

Despite the correlation between economic and political systems in a society, I insisted that Russia's political system was not finally and irrevocably determined in every detail and trend, and that this left some opportunities for opposing forces to work sensibly to adjust the system to actual challenges.

Indeed, I believed it possible to prevent the Russian political system from preserving its retrograde and stagnation-prone character for decades, to make it more flexible and reactive in dealing with the serious threats and difficulties it faces. As Russia's time horizon most probably stretches beyond the lifetime of its present political system, it is important to minimize the damage done to Russia's economy and future potential, even though this may help the system to survive longer than otherwise would be expected.

To accomplish this, I thought it necessary to organize and maintain powerful pressure from the roots of society, through public discussions and the use of the opportunities (however small they might be) provided by the remaining elements and rudiments of a free political system in Russia. For that very reason, I decided to take part in the presidential elections of 2018, knowing quite definitely that the system was impervious to any attempts by outsiders to change the planned scenario, let alone to win a potentially dangerous percentage of the popular vote. Indeed, I didn't even mind suffering a depressing defeat if that would make Russia's present rulers tone down their intolerance and take a more realistic look at Russia's present situation and future agenda. This attitude draws a line between responsible (and actually patriotic) opposition and those who are totally indifferent to the future lot of their country.

So what did we have during the past three years? The shortest answer would be "More of the same." I must admit that my cautious optimism with regard to possible changes in the system proved to be largely unfounded. Developments in Russia in recent years have not brought it any closer to the desirable U-turn or to a visible shift in major policy areas, and that is true of foreign policy as well as most domestic policy issues. On the contrary, signs have become more pronounced that Russia's autocracy is developing along the lines of long-term usurpation of power by a very close circle of people that see politics in terms of highly personal power play rather than as a mechanism to ensure the long-term survival of Russian statehood. Given the consequences of such a usurpation, in both the midterm and the long term the spectrum of remaining opportunities for change has become much narrower, at least for the next five to fifteen years.

Among all the recent changes since the book was originally written, I would highlight three in particular. The first is the increasingly strong reliance of Russia's autocracy on tight ideological pressure on society. I had written that stressing an officially imposed ideology was a relatively new phenomenon for Russia's postcommunist rulers. As recently as in the aughts, they preferred to abstain from developing a clear-cut official doctrine (or "national idea") that would be imposed on people by a powerful propaganda machine. Instead, they preferred vague ideals of "people's well-being," "steady development," and "might and prosperity," which would blur societal divisions and broaden the social base of the ruling regime. It was only in the early 2010s that patriotic rhetoric became increasingly xenophobic and nostalgic for the days of the Soviet "great empire," in geopolitical and cultural terms. In parallel, the regime has come to be treated as divine (God-given), indivisible from the idea of statehood, devoid of any internal divisions, and exclusive of control by laypeople.

By now these ideas have been officially codified as Russia's "traditional values," while the values of civil liberties, distribution of power between countervailing centers, mutual checks and balances, and the right of the governed to change their rulers have been declared alien to Russian traditions and subversive with regard to Russia's identity and security.

What makes things worse is that the official rhetoric of recent years has incorporated many elements of traditional Russian nationalism, such as the idea of a distinctly different "Russian civilization" (*Russkii mir*) that is antagonistic to Atlantic European civilization; the idea of the special historical mission of the Russian people, which presumes a right and duty to guide other nations in the form of benevolent empire; and the vision of the country's rulers as the central element and instrument of that mission rather than as a tool for maintaining daily life of its people to their benefit. By integrating into Russian nationalism certain leftist attitudes and approaches—such as a view of private property rights as conditional and secondary to national (state) rights, which are embodied in and established by the nation's rulers; animosity toward cosmopolitan global capital and business; and others—Russia's current rulers have managed to present Russia's ancient, imperial, Soviet, and post-Soviet history as an eternal fight for Russia's survival in a hostile, aggressive surrounding world that is eager to destroy Russian civilization and its intrinsic unity of the people with its rulers. In this context, the goal of raising standards of living and improving people's well-being is naturally replaced by the idea that people's lives are a tool in the mission of defending, "strengthening," and expanding Russian rule, which is the highest value.

The task of bringing this message home to ordinary people has been given to government-controlled media (first and foremost, federal TV broadcasters), educational establishments, the loyalist part of the Russian Orthodox Church, and non-Orthodox religious leaders. The task has been made easier by the increasing political and military confrontation with the West and by the inevitable concomitant growth of resentment and militaristic sentiment in public debate and the general atmosphere.

It is essential to keep in mind that these highly destructive elements of marginal thinking have been brought to the fore by the top authorities—by their conscious decision, which they falsely portray as a response to popular demand. In fact, the opposite is true: it is official and semi-official brainwashing that is poisoning the public with reactionary and obscurantist notions and attitudes, which the authorities then use to justify their rejection of European values and the modern concepts of self-ruled civil society.

The second notable change of recent years is the system's strong advance toward ridding itself of elements intrinsically alien to autocracy, such as political party pluralism, popular elections as a means of selecting people to fill government positions, or any instruments of external control over the activities of government officials. Since the last parliamentary elections, in 2016, Russia's media has visibly lost interest in party politics or elections to local legislative assemblies—the only venue that would give sense to political party activities, if those assemblies had any say in governing local affairs, which they seem to have lost.

The presidential election of 2018, if compared to previous elections, also marked one further step toward eliminating the air of competition among candidates. The election was designed and staged as a plebiscite, that is, as a confirmation of overwhelming public support for the only meaningful candidate worthy and capable of ruling the country, and for the system he embodies. It was planned by Putin's people that all the other candidates would be portrayed as showmen of sorts, recruited to make the event look a little bit colorful and amusing, with almost all of the participants playing by the book written by the presidential agencies in charge of the event.

In fact, these elections turned out to be an open demonstration of the understanding that Vladimir Putin derives his legitimacy not from the free choice of Russian citizens but by making them renounce their role in making key political decisions, including the choice of policies, in favor of the supreme leader, whom they cannot change but are invited to approve without debate or deliberation.

And yet I participated in the election, the plebiscite. Why, if the result was obvious from the start? Because, after nearly thirty years in Russian politics, I felt obliged to tell 110 million Russian voters what was really going on in the country. My task was not just to inform people about what was going on (in fact, the internet can do this perfectly, at least for those who truly want to be informed) but also to present an agenda for public debate and discussion, which would include issues that could be regarded as the most important for the future of the country.

These debates could not ignore the tens of thousands of victims of the war in Eastern Ukraine; the responsibility for the downing of a passenger Boeing in July of 2014; Ramzan Kadyrov's arbitrary rule in Chechnya, with its disrespect for human and civil rights; the annexation of Crimea; the war in Syria; or international economic sanctions.

The debates also should cover earlier events that formed Putin's political agenda, such as the second war in Chechnya, which helped him to attain the highest power; the terrible terrorist acts in Dubrovka and Beslan, which were not subject to thorough investigation, and the unprofessional actions of the authorities, which were responsible for the deaths of hundreds of hostages; the failure to bring to justice the murderers of many independent journalists, such as Yuri Shchekochikhin and Anna Politkovskaya; and the assassination of Boris Nemtsov.

Finally, public debate should not ignore the defeat of the Russian economy as a result of flaws in Putin's domestic and foreign policies, the issue of mass poverty, or the complete nondelivery on authorities' promises.

My participation in the presidential election campaign, despite the fake nature of the proceedings, gave me an opportunity to discuss these issues at mass meetings with voters, to make my ideas heard by millions of people during TV debates, and to present them in my campaign materials. It may very well be that this was the last opportunity to deliver on a national scale such messages about the plight of the country and to propose remedies to avert the looming crisis. I felt obliged to use this last chance. Television stations and other mass media controlled by Putin's system were opened to opposing views for only a short period during the official election campaign, and I reasoned that this short period of open opportunity should be utilized to its fullest.

The number of votes I gathered, according to official results, was rather small. Nevertheless, I am sure that I succeeded in planting in the minds of millions of my fellow countrymen the seeds of serious deliberation on their future and the future of their children, and I am sure that, in time, these seeds will grow and Russia will return to the path of freedom.

The official results of the 2018 elections could hardly be interpreted as active support of Putin's rule by the majority of the population, but they are and will be used by the authorities as evidence that Russia's people see no alternative to this rule. This could become a sort of milestone on the way to transforming the current authoritarian regime into a postmodern totalitarian system, if the authorities choose to proceed in this direction.

The third marked change that we have witnessed during the past three years is the system's increased personalism, by which I mean the elimination of any checks on the personal power of the top man in the state's command hierarchy. As a result of years of devolution, the system now consists of no institution or position that could possibly exercise control over decisions made by the top ruler, something like the Soviet-era Communist Party Politburo. Since recovering his presidential post in 2012, Vladimir Putin not only has exercised rigid control over all branches of government, including its legislative and judicial bodies, but also has deprived consultative bodies like the Security Council of the ability to influence key decisions, which are developed and finalized at Putin's own discretion. The process of decision-making has been closed to both the general public and the members of the political establishment, who, like the general public, seem to have few available sources of related important information. In terms of policy-making and policy debate, the bodies of the formally ruling United Russia Party have turned into the same kind of phantom institutions as the "opposition" parties represented in parliament.

Finally, it could be argued that recent developments have made it nearly impossible for external actors to influence political decision-making or political activities in Russia. On the one hand, this is the result of the actions of the Russian authorities, who strove to limit such possibilities through more far-reaching and exhaustive regulation and restriction of foreign actors in all social and public activities inside Russia. A growing number of nongovernmental organizations and media outlets with foreign participation or sponsorship have been subject to strict control, overt trolling, or outright bans on their activities. As the authorities gradually abandoned the idea of maintaining a good reputation with Western or Western-dominated international institutions, those organizations lost both direct and indirect leverage with regard to Russian activities and behavior.

Furthermore, the Russian authorities have learned to turn attempted outside pressure to their benefit in domestic propaganda. For example, the United Kingdom's accusation that Russian authorities were behind the poisoning of former Russian agent Sergei Skripal and his daughter was used to stir up support for Putin on the eve of the March 2018 elections.

At the same time, foreign powers have abandoned the idea of attempting to influence Putin's domestic policy and have left it completely to Putin's discretion. Western actions, which are viewed by Russia's government as hostile, are designed either to prevent the Kremlin from using external resources and opportunities to its own ends or to prevent it from making particular steps in its foreign policy, while domestic policy has come to be regarded by the West as the Kremlin's exclusive prerogative.

On the whole, the Putin system has acquired the features of a mature autocracy organized on the principles of Mafia-like syndicates, with personal rule, a sophisticated ideological underpinning, and steady support from below, while external threats to it have been reduced to a minimal level.

The results of the March 18, 2018, plebiscite opened the way for Putin's lifelong rule. In fact, that was its main purpose, determined by the ruling circle. The technical details of implementing this task, including possible changes to relevant clauses of the constitution, evidently will be decided upon later, depending on the balance of different powers and groups within the Kremlin. It makes little sense to attempt to guess which scenario will finally be chosen—though, in any of them, the resources of the system will sooner or later be exhausted, if only because of the physical limits of human life.

But Putin's system cannot last forever for a bigger reason: its built-in deficiencies will prevent it from maintaining continuous control over political and business life. Even before its lower links fly out of control, members of the ruling circle will become aware of the looming crisis and the need for change. Inevitably, that will require either a deep review of the system (which would be the minimum change needed) or a reform of political life on completely different principles, which would also invite radical changes in business life.

However, before that happens, the system will have to travel the entire road from supposed triumph to actual collapse. And Russia will have to travel the path along with the system, no matter how distressing that may be. Moreover, the question of what system would replace the current one remains open. If it is a hybrid version of the Soviet system or a techno-military dictatorship, Russia's prospects will be dim indeed.

To prevent that outcome requires a lot of hard work. By the time Russia approaches the next fork in the road, there must be well-educated and politically acute people ready to use the moment of truth to reinstate necessary political institutions. That's why I thought it necessary and important to take the opportunity to talk to the nation as a presidential candidate in the recent campaign. We must work for the future by cultivating the soil for a forthcoming new politics in Russia.

NOTES

PREFACE TO THE ENGLISH TRANSLATION

1. This data is taken from Capgemini, *The Wealth Reports*, http://www.worldwealthreport.com. Accessed August 13, 2018.
2. Robert D. Putnam, *Bowling Alone: The Collapse and Revival of American Community* (New York: Simon and Schuster, 2000).

1. THE POLITICAL SYSTEM OF PUTIN'S RUSSIA AND ITS SIGNIFICANCE FOR WORLD AFFAIRS

1. G. A. Yavlinsky, *Rossiiskaia ekonomicheskaia sistema: Nastoiashchee i budushchee* [The Russian Economic System: Today and Tomorrow] (Moscow: Medium, 2007). See also Grigory Yavlinsky, "Russia's Phony Capitalism," *Foreign Affairs*, May/June 1998; Sergei Braguinsky and Grigory Yavlinsky, *Incentives and Institutions: The Transition to a Market Economy in Russia* (Princeton, N.J.: Princeton University Press, 2000); and Grigory Yavlinsky, *Realeconomik: The Hidden Cause of the Great Recession (and How to Avert the Next One)* (New Haven, Conn.: Yale University Press, 2011).
2. See, for example, Grigory Yavlinsky, *Periferiinyi kapitalizm* [Peripheral Capitalism] (Moscow: EPIcenter, 2003); or *Perspektivy Rossii: Ekonomicheskii i politicheskii vzgliad* [Russia's Prospects: An Economic and Political View] (Moscow: Galleia-print, 2006).
3. See, for example, my article in *Voprosy ekonomiki* [Economic Affairs] 9 (2007): 19–26.

2. RUSSIA TODAY: THE HISTORY OF HOW AND WHY IT CAME TO BE

1. Mancur Olson, *Power and Prosperity: Outgrowing Communist and Capitalist Dictatorships* (New York: Basic Books, 2000).
2. For an extensive if not an exhaustive list of such hypotheses, see, for example, Sergey Guriyev and Oleg Tsyvinsky, "*Ratio economica*: Demokratichnyi krizis," *Vedomosti* 161 (3175), August 28, 2012.
3. In the course of the twentieth century such authoritarian regimes, sometimes dubbed "developmental dictatorships" in Western literature, viewed themselves through the prism of their attempts to pull their countries out of economic backwardness and to try to catch up with the developed core of the world economy, or even to join it. The Soviet Union can apparently be considered one of those "developmental dictatorships," at least at some stages of its historical trajectory.
4. Interview with Robert Aumann, *Vedomosti* 121 (3135), July 3, 2012; Daron Acemoglu and James A. Robinson, *Economic Origins of Dictatorship and Democracy* (Cambridge, Mass.: Harvard University Press, 2006); Acemoglu and Robinson, *Why Nations Fail: The Origins of Power, Prosperity, and Poverty* (London: Profile, 2012).
5. In the fall of 1991, I drafted an agreement on the economic union of the newly independent states—the former Soviet republics. That treaty envisioned the preservation of a joint currency, the establishment of a free trade zone, a joint customs control, continued cooperation among factories and firms of the former Soviet Union, harmonization of economic legislation across these countries, and other measures. The treaty was signed at the highest level of the Kremlin, with the participation of Mikhail Gorbachev and representatives of the leadership of thirteen out of fifteen former Soviet republics, including Ukraine and Kazakhstan (and with the exception of Azerbaijan and Georgia). The Baltic states also signed that treaty as observers. More than sixty rule-making acts needed for the implementation of this treaty were prepared and approved by the governments of the signatory states. However, the Belaya Vezha agreements on disbanding the union made it impossible to continue this work.
6. On a more general level, it is worth noting in this regard that the meaning of elections as a political institution greatly depends not only

upon the integrity of electoral procedure, however important it is, but also upon the outcome of the elections—the character of the resulting change in the shape of power relationships. One possibility is that elections result in a limited but not a radical shift in these power relationships. That is, the side that wins the elections gets the opportunity to fill some government offices but does not obtain all power in its entirety; the losing party retains its power in other branches and at other levels of government, as well as their access to the media and the opportunity to successfully use the courts to challenge the decisions made by the winning party, among other things. But if the winner takes all without leaving anything to the defeated party, it is a different situation altogether. In other words, behind the seemingly uniform institution of elections, one can find fundamentally different principles of organization of power.

7. See Grigory Yavlinsky, *Realeconomik: The Hidden Cause of the Great Recession (and How to Avert the Next One)* (New Haven, Conn.: Yale University Press, 2011).
8. Yavlinsky, *Realeconomik*.
9. In the first years of the twenty-first century, Russia's economic system began absorbing very large windfall profits from the export of raw materials and hydrocarbons. These superprofits greatly reinforced and accelerated its political consolidation. The most significant stages of this process were as follows:

    - the subordination of all politically influential media, with the destruction of the NTV media company (2000–2002);
    - the deepening fusion of government power with the ownership of economic assets through an even greater subordination of businesses to the state, with President Putin's tight personal control of all financial flows and the shrinking of the private sector of the economy (as exemplified by the prosecution of Yukos from 2003 on);
    - the elimination of all autonomy whatsoever for regional elites, with the abolition of gubernatorial elections (2002);
    - the unleashing of no-holds-barred propaganda in government-owned media; the reversal of the editorial policies of the previously influential democratic mass media through semi-involuntary

transfers of their ownership rights to the largest government-owned public companies; the transformation of these media into tools of the ruling circle, serving their interests by manipulating public opinion (first and foremost the opinion of the educated class in Moscow and Saint Petersburg); and a drastic increase in the scale of election fraud (starting in 2003);

- the intimidation of society, beginning in 2012, including intimidation of young people (with the prosecution of the band Pussy Riot), of protest rally participants (with the prosecution of the Bolotnaya Square protesters), of human rights advocates and civic organizations (with the "foreign agent" labeling, in accordance with the newly passed law), and of the bureaucracy (with the prosecution of the former Defense Minister Anatoly Serdyukov); loud campaigns targeting various minorities (such as the campaign against "homosexual propaganda"); the campaign for the "nationalization of the elite"; and other actions; and
- active efforts to create a pervasive sense of a lack of alternatives to the status quo, regardless of the quality and the mistakes of the power holders.

10. Let me quote here an editorial published on August 16, 2013, by *Vedomosti*, Russia's leading business paper: "The situation that we have with the ownership of large economic assets stinks. The holdings acquired in the course of privatization were not earned by their present owners. The transfer of property rights to the new owners of factories and coal mines looked like the return to a state of injustice and had a tinge of a royal grant in exchange for loyalty. . . . The government retains an implicit 'golden share' in large property holdings, especially in those that the Kremlin views as having a strategic value."
11. Many observers have noted that, during the entire period of Mikhail Khodorkovsky's imprisonment (and he explicitly confirmed it after his release), his confrontation with the government, in political terms, did not suggest—either then or today—an opposite or a fundamentally different direction for Russia's development than the one that has been pursued by the Kremlin.
12. In actuality, private and government funds allocated by Western countries for "global democracy support" were rather limited, and even

these funds were typically spent on personally enriching "professional democratizers," with payments having rather tenuous connection to the actual outcomes of their work. The practical result of this "struggle for democracy," in the West, was sustained public attention to a few dozen media stories and personalities whose high profiles were out of sync with their actual significance and impact in terms of power relationships in Russia, which was minimal at best.

3. AUTHORITARIANISM ON THE PERIPHERY: UNDERSTANDING RUSSIA'S POLITICAL SYSTEM AND HOW IT WORKS

1. This aspect of the situation is rarely mentioned, and yet it is critically important. The authorities cannot completely protect themselves against scathing critiques and outright invective. Mass access to the internet makes this physically and technically impossible—as developments in China have demonstrated, controlling discussions on the internet is not feasible even with much more rigid and effective surveillance of the population. Therefore, manipulating public opinion becomes the most potent means of counteracting criticism. Major mass media as well as the "niche" opposition outlets largely neutralize critics of the system by pushing to the fore issues and stories that appear inconsequential or preposterous to most of the country's population. This may be done either intentionally or because of the outlets' extremely low professional standards. The achievement of this goal is further simplified by the attitudes of a large part of the opposition-minded intelligentsia: viewing themselves as part and parcel of the global (Western) elite, they feel that they don't have to take into consideration the needs, beliefs, tastes, and prejudices of the bulk of the population (which they brand "bumpkins," "rednecks," and holdovers from the Soviet era). As a result, instead of presenting issues that might animate the masses (such as the condition of the social safety net, the performance of the judiciary and law enforcement agencies, health care, and education), the agenda of the system's critics gets filled with discussions of the personal ups and downs of individual oppositionists, infringements upon individual artists' freedom of creativity, and other stories that cause a mixed and skeptical response

among the depoliticized majority of Russians. The role of the politicized intelligentsia of Moscow and Saint Petersburg in the emergence, development, and consolidation of the system of peripheral authoritarianism in Russia deserves a separate and fairly blunt appraisal.

2. It is telling that, in their pronouncements, genuine supporters of the authoritarian system do not count the political parties represented in the Duma as opposition but, by default, as part and parcel of the national elite, consolidated around its official leader. See, for example, Grigory Dobromelov, "Two Years of Castling," *Expert* [in Russian], September 24, 2013, http://expert.ru/2013/09/24/dva-goda-rokirovki.
3. In theory, an external threat can also play the role of such a constraint, but it has to be grave, tangible, and immediate. In present-day conditions, such situations occur infrequently, and it is even more rare for a ruling group to perceive them as such. Evidence shows that authoritarian regimes direct much more attention and resources toward preventing the emergence of potential domestic threats (such as riots, uncontrollable outbursts of violence and disobedience, or organized opposition) and toward fighting external opponents who are not among the most dangerous than toward protecting their countries against potential invasion by those who may actually pose such a risk.
4. I am talking here not about ideology in its broader sense, as an element of the social consciousness of a community of people, but rather about specific ideological systems that serve as political tools.
5. I will not discuss here the extent to which the principles on which Russia's new economic system was being built were actually market-based. I addressed this subject in many of my prior works.
6. Some Russian commentators explain "strong power," as understood by the present ruling circle, as being independent of the society it governs. This is also true. However, the main distinctive feature of a strong power, from the Kremlin's point of view, is its ability to suppress any threats to its capacity to govern and any doubts regarding its right to do so.
7. We should keep in mind that the West is not merely a convenient propaganda target. It is in fact dangerous for Russia's ruling circle, first

and foremost because it symbolizes those principles that are most dangerous and destructive for Russia's peripheral authoritarian regime—namely, the principle of equality before the law, the principle of an independent judiciary, the inviolability of private property, and the ideal of holding government accountable to society.

8. I am not the only one to observe these ideological trends. The list of interviews, blogs, and other publications by fairly prominent members of Russia's political establishment, and by its dispassionate analysts, that make note of the ideological bent of the authorities, beginning around 2012–2013, would be pretty long.
9. The same principle was used in Soviet central planning under Joseph Stalin: the targets set in the plans were known to be impossible to meet, yet the punishments for failing to meet them were applied selectively, depending on one's political preferences and the currently ongoing propagandistic campaigns.
10. Prominent sociologist Immanuel Wallerstein (at Yale University), writing with Georgi Derluguian, describes the present-day division between the core zone of global capitalism and its periphery as akin to a solar system, in which every country is a planet orbiting around the sun—the "core" of the system—each at its own distance from it. Under certain circumstances, some of these country-planets may either move up to an orbit closer to the sun or slip into a more distant orbit. Georgi Derluguian and Immanuel Wallerstein, *A Story of a Downfall: The Soviet Civilization Project in the Context of Global History*, *Expert* 1, no. 784 (December 26, 2011) [in Russian].
11. See, for example, Francis Fukuyama, "The Future of History: Can Liberal Democracy Survive the Decline of the Middle Class?," *Foreign Affairs* 9, no. 1 (January/February 2012), https://www.foreignaffairs.com/articles/2012-01-01/future-history.
12. While these raises have been very modest in absolute terms, they give the impression that the Kremlin views raising public sector wages as its priority.
13. Among the former Soviet countries, there have already been several examples of a situation in which a functioning parliament turned out to be the last resort in preventing the country from slipping into actual chaos and anarchy when it was faced with an acute crisis of

governability and the executive hierarchy's loss of control over the state of affairs.

4. THE FUTURE OF AUTOCRACY IN RUSSIA: WHAT DO WE HAVE TO TOLERATE (AND FOR HOW LONG)?

1. The lively academic debate spurred by the works of Samuel Huntington and the concepts that he put forward is an example of such a legitimation of this theory. See, for example, Huntington, *The Clash of Civilizations and the Remaking of World Order* (New York: Simon and Schuster, 1996).
2. Grigory Yavlinsky, *Realeconomik: The Hidden Cause of the Great Recession (and How to Avert the Next One)* (New Haven, Conn.: Yale University Press, 2011).
3. I intentionally use the word "Ukraine" without the article "the" for political reasons.
4. As Putin expressed it, in his remarks in the Kremlin about the Crimean situation, "Russia felt that it had not been just robbed but that it had been plundered." Vladimir Putin, "Address of the President of the Russian Federation" [in Russian], Kremlin.ru, March 18, 2014, http://www.kremlin.ru/events/president/news/20603
5. These elements include a nostalgic, idealized notion of the Soviet system; of the autocratic police state that existed under Tsar Nicholas I (1825–1855); of the counterreforms of the 1880s; of the notorious "freezing" of Russia in the 1890s, associated with the name of the influential courtier Konstantin Pobedonostsev; and even of the "lessons" of Russia's abrupt territorial expansion under Ivan the Terrible and Peter the Great, which coincided with brutal transformations of the country against its will. And to make all this look smart, government propaganda generously peppers this eclectic mix with quotations from various Russian philosophers of the early twentieth century (known as the "Silver Age" of Russia's culture), from Ivan Ilyin to Nikolai Berdyaev. These quotations tend to be taken completely out of any context to which they originally belonged.

INDEX